I0824197

PRAISE FOR G-QUE BARBEQUE

"I often say I know everybody and their brother in the BBQ world. When I think of Colorado BBQ, Jason and G-Que are always my first thoughts. At Meat Church, it's all about bringing people together to make great memories around great food—and Jason is doing exactly that with this book. With his knowledge and recipes, he's about to take you to church!"

—Matt Pittman, Meat Church BBQ

"When I was on the field, the goal was always domination. Jason brings that same intensity to the BBQ game. This book is pure championship smoke—recipes that hit harder than a goal-line stand and flavors that'll have you chest-bumping your smoker. His playbook is stacked. This isn't just a cookbook; it's a game plan for greatness—and every backyard needs it."

—Derek Wolfe, Super Bowl Champion,
Sack Master, and BBQ Hype Man

"Whether you're a backyard cook, competitor, or restaurateur, this book delivers. Jason not only shares the secret to his success—building a strong team—but also serves up recipes you can use for both backyard grilling and large catering events. Honestly, I can't decide if this is a motivational book or a cookbook, because you get the best of both in one. It's well written, inspiring, and the food looks so good you'll have a hard time not licking the pages."

—Darren Warth, 15-Time World Champion,
Owner of Smokey D's BBQ, Des Moines, IA

G-QUE
CHAMPIONSHIP BARBEQUE

G-QUE BARBEQUE

A MILE ABOVE THE REST

MORE THAN 75 PROVEN RECIPES FOR BREAKING BARBEQUE BOUNDARIES

CHAMPIONSHIP-WINNING PITMASTER

JASON GANAHL

WITH

JAMES O. FRAIOLI

Skyhorse Publishing

Food photography by Ken Goodman Photography
Additional photography by Jason Ganahl and G-Que Barbeque, and Shutterstock

Skyhorse Publishing books may be purchased in bulk at special discounts for sales promotion, corporate gifts, fund-raising, or educational purposes. Special editions can also be created to specifications. For details, contact the Special Sales Department, Skyhorse Publishing, 307 West 36th Street, 11th Floor, New York, NY 10018 or info@skyhorsepublishing.com.

Skyhorse® and Skyhorse Publishing® are registered trademarks of Skyhorse Publishing, Inc.®, a Delaware corporation.

Visit our website at www.skyhorsepublishing.com.

Culinary Book Creations LLC
www.culinarybookcreations.com

10 9 8 7 6 5 4 3 2 1

Library of Congress Cataloging-in-Publication Data on file.

Cover design by theBookDesigners
Cover photo credit: Ken Goodman Photography

Hardcover ISBN: 978-1-5107-8539-7
Ebook ISBN: 978-1-5107-8666-0

Printed in China

To God and everyone who believed in G-Que Barbeque— the guests who craved it, the team who brought it to life, and the friends who spread the word. You are the heart and soul of this journey. I couldn't do it without you.

JASON GANAHL

G-QUE BBQ
G-QUE
CHAMPIONSHIP BARBEQUE
COLORADO'S ONLY
SHIP BBQ
ALASKA
SCAN HERE
FOR A FREE
PULLED PORK
SANDWICH
GQUEBBQ.COM
HOME OF THE $1 BEER
MONDAY – FRIDAY | 2-5PM
COLORADO'S BEST HAPPY HOUR!

GQue BBQ
Colorado Est 2015

CUTS
ELLENCE
LENTLESS
UNTLESS
NSHIPS,
ED
S OUR CRAFT,
S OUR PURPOSE.
-QUE.

COLORADO COWS
MAKE THE BEST
Ice Cream
EXIT
G-QUE

I BB

CONTENTS

RECIPES: ELEVATED SPECIALS

THE ROOTS OF G-QUE BARBEQUE

Let me take you back to where it all began— because every great journey starts with a moment of doubt, but it's those moments that define who we become.

My culinary journey didn't start with barbeque; it began humbly at Garavellis Café in St. Louis, Missouri, when I was fourteen years old. Back then, I landed my first job washing dishes for $3.75 an hour. It might not sound like much now, but to a fourteen-year-old with no financial obligations, it was everything. Neither of my parents went to college, and no one in my family before them did, so the idea of working hard and earning my own money was a source of pride and satisfaction for me.

I remember thinking, "If I can find a way to make $4 an hour, I'll be rich!"—the simple dreams of a teenager without rent or bills to worry about. That mindset quickly shifted when I worked my way up to busboy, where I shared in a tip pool from the floor hosts. It was in this role that I learned one of the most valuable lessons of my life: the more value I could create for others, the more I could earn.

Through my teens and into my early 20s, I worked a variety of restaurant jobs. I gravitated toward front-of-house roles like serving and bartending because of the tips. I loved the challenge of surpassing guests' expectations, creating a memorable experience for them in exchange for higher tips. It was always about creating value, about going above and beyond.

I honed my hospitality chops working for tips for eight years, and it wasn't until I started living on my own that I learned how to cook. In my mid-20s, eating out all the time wasn't an option—I simply couldn't afford it. Not just eating but eating good has always been one of my favorite things to do, so I began teaching myself how to cook.

I learned to make the most out of simple, inexpensive ingredients, focusing on seasoning them properly and mastering techniques like braising, sautéing, and roasting. Back then, I watched the Food Network religiously, absorbing everything I could from my favorite chefs: Bobby Flay and Ina Garten. This was well before the age of YouTube, and I wasn't into reading cookbooks yet, so Food Network became my go-to teacher.

Having majored in Biology, I found that my scientific background was incredibly helpful in learning to cook. Understanding the science behind food—why certain things happen or don't happen in the cooking process—allowed me to test hypotheses and develop my skills. That foundation would become key when I later dove into creating and perfecting winning barbeque recipes.

After working in restaurants for as long as I did, I realized that the customer service skills I had honed over the years could be applied to sales. I enjoyed creating value for people, and helping others brought me a lot of joy, so I believed I could excel in sales. Turns out, I was right. I found success in sales, and that opened opportunities for me—but it also meant moving away from home.

I first moved to San Ramon, California, working in Pleasanton while continuing to build my career. Eventually, I was offered a position in Boulder, Colorado, working for what was then Tyco (now Medtronic), where I held a variety of sales and marketing management positions. Those roles taught me so much about business—lessons that I would later apply to G-Que Barbeque. From understanding how to market a product to leading teams and managing vendors, my experiences in leadership became invaluable assets. As I look back on this time what I learned most was not to want things to be easier but to learn skills to help overcome the obstacles. Whether it's not getting defensive, building trust, communicating effectively, or analyzing data, the more skills you can acquire or the more you can improve the skills you have, you can achieve the outcomes you want instead of wishing for things to just be easier. This confidence is what allowed me to start a business in the medical device space before I had G-Que.

While I lived in St. Louis, I ate barbeque regularly. Back then, places like Sugarfire and Pappy's didn't exist yet, but my go-to spot was Bandana's Barbeque. I wasn't a barbeque snob by any means—if it was smoked right and not over-seasoned, I was happy. I loved the flavor that smoking meat infused, a taste of hickory that couldn't be replicated in an oven or frying pan.

When I moved to California, I found a few barbeque places that I enjoyed, but it wasn't until I moved to Colorado that I really started searching for something special. That search led me to discover the Kansas City Barbeque Society (KCBS), and I learned that they hosted professional barbeque contests. I thought, "This is interesting. I have to learn more about this." So, I attended my first professional barbeque contest as a spectator—and that's where everything started to change.

I was just a spectator that day, excited to try what I thought would be some of the best barbeque I'd ever had. There was live music, barbeque aromas filled the air, the hair on the back of my neck stood up. Cold beer, hot barbeque, and everyone was smiling—I found my people! The very first vendor I visited, I took a bite of his ribs, and I was blown away. "These are the best ribs I've ever tasted!" I thought. My expectations skyrocketed. This vendor must be one of the top teams, surely. When the results came in later that day, I couldn't believe what I saw—he finished 59th out of 65 teams.

It was a shock. If these were the best ribs I'd ever tasted, and he finished almost last, what chance did I have? Could I ever compete in this world? It felt like an impossible hill to climb. That self-doubt can creep in early and if you let it, it will stick around and remind you that you have no shot to become what you're capable of becoming.

After that first contest as a spectator, despite the self-doubt, I knew I wanted to be a part of the community. My barbeque skills at the time were nowhere near where they needed to be. If I wanted to compete, hoping that it would be easy wasn't going to cut it—I needed to improve, to truly understand what made barbeque great. So, I made a decision that would shape everything that came next. I became a Certified Barbeque Judge.

For two years, I judged competitions, sitting under the tent with the best of the best, tasting barbeque that people had poured their hearts and souls into. And let me tell you something, the best barbeque you'll ever eat isn't from a restaurant—it's under that KCBS judges' tent. Judging allowed me to see, taste, and experience what barbeque excellence looked like. But more importantly, it gave me insight into how judges think, what they're looking for when they evaluate an entry, and what sets the top competitors apart from the rest. After those two years of tasting all that competition barbeque and practicing at home, I was ready. It was time to stop sitting on the sidelines and start competing.

THE FIRST BARBEQUE COMPETITION: PUEBLO, COLORADO

I entered my first barbeque contest in Pueblo, Colorado, down by the riverwalk. It was a humble start—I rented a U-Haul, loaded my smoker, and drove down to compete against 60 other teams. My setup was anything but glamorous. While the other teams rolled in with trailers and RVs, I was tucked away at the end, far from the polished, professional setups. I knew no one. Most of my relationships were with judges, and they didn't arrive until it was time to score the entries on Saturday.

I was a one-man team—while most competitors had a crew to handle different tasks, I had to figure out everything on my own. I even forgot to bring a light, which meant working through the night in the dark. That contest was full of lessons, but none bigger than perseverance. There were multiple times I thought, *What the heck am I doing here?*

Eventually, my wife's friend from high school, Molly, had a husband named Kenny who became part of the team. My wife Heidi would share with Molly what I was doing competing in barbeque contests, and Kenny inquired about joining me, knowing that I could use help. He became my go-to guy, always making sure I had a cold beer in hand and helping me with the operational side of things so I could focus on the cooking. He made it to about 20% of the contests, usually the bigger ones, but those times together were priceless. We laughed a lot and had some of the best times competing side by side. Sadly, he passed away a few years ago doing something he loved—running a Spartan Race—and I miss him dearly to this day.

At KCBS contests, you turn in four meats: Chicken, Ribs, Pork, and Brisket. And then there's the overall ranking, where the ultimate goal is to be crowned the Grand Champion. That's what every competitor dreams of.

For all the mishaps of that first contest, I'll never forget when my name was called—twice, inside the top 10, in two categories. That rush of excitement and validation were indescribable. Doubling down on the emotion I was feeling in that moment, I made a commitment to myself that I wasn't just going to compete—I was going to win. First, I set my sights on winning a category, then a Grand Championship, and ultimately, the Rocky Mountain Barbeque Association (RMBBQA) Team of the Year award, which goes to the best team across nine states, and 30 contests over the course of a year.

PITS
CAPE GIRARDEAU,

THE RISE OF G-QUE BARBEQUE: 19 GRAND AND RESERVED GRAND CHAMPIONSHIPS AND RMBBQA TEAM OF THE YEAR AND HALL OF FAME INDUCTEE

In the years that followed, in my free time, I put everything I had into perfecting my barbeque skills. I read every barbeque book I could get my hands on, practiced constantly, and honed my craft. It wasn't about trying my best and *hoping* to do good—it was about relentless dedication. I did what it took to win, and over time, I started winning. The wins were a byproduct of the effort. I put in the work during the week and collected the trophies on the weekend—countless category wins and 19 Grand or Reserve Grand Championships.

And in 2014, I achieved what I set out to do: RMBBQA Team of the Year, after narrowly missing it in 2013 to Burning Bob! I credit Burning Bob with much of my competitive barbeque success. He was my fiercest competitor. A retired United Airlines mechanic with a trophy room stocked full of Grand Championships. To be the best you must beat the best, and Bob set the bar high. Thank you, Bob, for never letting up. You are one of the fiercest competitors I know.

Every contest, every challenge was an opportunity to grow, to learn, to become better. Because in barbeque, like in life, success isn't a destination. It's a journey, and that journey is about far more than trophies or titles.

What I've come to realize is that the true reward isn't the recognition or the accolades—it's who you become in the process. Every challenge you face, every setback, every moment of doubt is a test, a chance to build yourself into someone stronger, more resilient, and more capable than you were before.

When you're thinking to yourself, *This isn't for me, I should just quit and find something else to do*, the resistance to not quit is when the real growth happens. It's in those moments that you learn what you're made of. You either give up, or you dig deep, push through the self-doubt, and find the strength to keep going. That's where you evolve.

Nothing worthwhile comes easy. Each time I faced a tough cook, an unexpected setback, or a fierce competitor, I didn't just become a better pitmaster—I became a better version of myself. Because overcoming challenges is what shapes you. It builds the kind of mental toughness that spills over into every other area of your life.

The journey has taught me that success isn't about avoiding failure or adversity—it's about confronting it head-on. Every setback is a stepping stone, every failure is a lesson in disguise. You don't just become great by winning, you become great by enduring the struggle, by learning from every mistake, by persevering when others would quit. There were several times I wanted to quit. The more you push yourself through those moments of doubt and difficulty, the more you start to see challenges not as roadblocks but as opportunities to prove to yourself what you're capable of. That's what barbeque taught me—and that's what I apply to every aspect of my life. The rewards of the journey are found in who you become when you refuse to quit, when you refuse to settle, and when you constantly strive for more.

OPENING G-QUE BARBEQUE: A LEAP OF FAITH

Despite all my success on the competition barbeque circuit, I was reluctant to open a restaurant. Self-doubt was looking me right in the face telling me it owns me! You hear it all the time—how hard the restaurant business is. The long hours, the struggle to make money, the endless challenges. And it's true. Owning a restaurant requires sacrifice, especially in the beginning. At the time, my wife Heidi and I were just starting our family. It was easy for me to come up with reasons not to start a restaurant.

But Heidi saw something in me that I was hesitant to acknowledge. She gave me the nudge I needed and told me, "If you're going to do it, it's time." Hearing her say that made it more than about me—it was about the team I would build and the community we would serve. It was a chance to demonstrate to my family that they can count on me. Her believing in me meant so much to me at a time when I didn't believe in myself.

I began networking with people in the industry, connecting with those who had already walked the path. I had a few key individuals who were incredibly generous with their time, sharing the lessons they'd learned, the mistakes they'd made, and the advice they wished someone had given them when they first started.

I put together a financial forecast, gathering assumptions and data from these experienced folks, and projected the numbers five years into the future. But here's the thing—the best-case scenario I came up with wasn't exactly comforting. In fact, it was hard to justify moving forward. The startup costs were high, and the numbers weren't just about replacing my income—I had to recoup my initial investment too.

On paper, the decision didn't make sense. I wasn't just opening any restaurant; I was taking over a failed pizza shop that had struggled as did every other previous tenant. The space had no visibility to traffic, parking was a nightmare, and to hit my projections, we would need to do five times the sales of the last tenant just to break even. As a first time restaurateur with a very limited budget and a desire to stay close to home I had very few options as landlords were not lining up to have people like me as tenants.

It was a leap that defied logic.

It obviously wasn't the forecast or the spreadsheets that convinced me to move forward. Somehow, I knew we would outperform any projections. In hindsight, it was faith that what I was doing had a greater purpose. Faith that this venture was part of a bigger plan, one that extended beyond the numbers. Of course, at the time, you could say it was a healthy case of naiveté. I remember a couple days before opening, I didn't sleep at all, thinking I made the worse decision of my life by signing a lease and expecting to do numbers that no one thinks is possible.

But faith, to me, is believing in something when the evidence suggests a different outcome. And when I look back, I credit my decision to open G-Que to that faith. Even in my moments of doubt, I continued. God was at work doing only what He can do and that's what made it successful. The vision He had was bigger than just opening a restaurant. It was about creating something that would serve others, something that would have a lasting impact.

The courage to take that leap didn't come from certainty—it came from trusting in something greater. I knew the road ahead would be difficult, but I also knew that we were meant to do more than just survive. We were meant to thrive. And in that moment, I embraced the uncertainty, knowing that we could accomplish, create, and serve in ways unknown to me at the time.

G-QUE BARBEQUE: THE FIRST DAY AND THE ROAD TO GROWTH

After nearly a year of preparation—finding time whenever I could to do what needed to be done to open a restaurant—the big day finally arrived. Opening day at G-Que Barbeque was here. We were operating on a barebones budget, but we had something more valuable than money: heart and hustle. The doors opened, and there was a line of people ready to come in, excited to see what we were about. But here's the thing—the staff and I weren't ready for it.

Like my first barbeque competition, that first day was packed with learning opportunities. We were struggling, and I'll never forget it. Some friends had come in for lunch, and seeing how we were falling behind, Mark Strachan and his family jumped into the kitchen without me even asking. They just knew. They saw the need, and they took action.

2014
GRAND CHAMPION
WILD WEST BBQ
BBQ CHALLENGE
1ST BRISKET
North Platte
HONKY TONK BARBECUE
Festival
GRAND CHAMPION
KCBS
KANSAS CITY BARBEQUE SOCIETY
Sam's CLUB
Sam's Club
NATIONAL BBQ TOUR
2013
1st Place
Chicken
Las Vegas, NV Regional
Sam's Club
NATIONAL BBQ TOUR
2013
1st Place
Ribs
Las Vegas, NV Regional
North Platte
HONKY TONK
BARBECUE
Festival
Rocky Mountain Freedom Festival
Castle Rock, Colorado
July 2, 2011

Pitmaster competes for national title
Daily Camera
HONKY TONK BARBECUE Festival
GRAND CHAMPION
NORTH PLATTE
HONKY TONK
PRESENTED BY
SECOND PLACE RIBS
SMOKIN' ON THE PRAIRIE
MBBQA Chicken
BBQ
Sam's Club
NATIONAL BBQ TOUR
2012
2nd Place
Sam's CLUB
North Platte
HONKY TONK BARBECUE Festival
FIRST PLACE BRISKET
NORTH PLATTE
GQUE
ROCKY MOUNTAIN

EXIT
G-QUE
ICE CREAM
Key Lime Pie
PARK

Operationally it was as bad as it could get. We had no time to do a friends and family or soft opening as I was already paying rent and had little money to float; we had to open, and we felt the consequences of being unprepared. We had only one way to go: up. From that day forward, we got better, a little bit each day. And here's what most people don't realize—those small improvements compound over time. After about a year, we finally started to figure out what we were doing, and things began to take off.

As we grew, I kept hearing the same thing from people: "You need to open a location in South Denver!" Our first location was in North Denver, and people down south wanted a taste of what we were serving. So, I listened, and I did it. I opened a second location in Lone Tree.

Where were all those people that told me they wanted a G-Que by them down south? When we opened, no one showed up. I thought everyone who said don't open a second restaurant was right.

I have a vivid memory of standing in the dining room during the first week at 6:30 p.m., looking around at the empty tables, thinking, "What did I get myself into?" It was a humbling moment. I wanted it to be easier this second time around, but it wasn't. The brand was unknown down south, and I had to apply all the same tactics and strategies that made the first G-Que a success. It was like starting over from scratch except I had a playbook of what works from our first location in Westminster.

And here's the kicker—I wasn't just opening a barbeque restaurant. I launched a homemade ice cream shop right next door featuring the best dairy I could find in Colorado. Why ice cream? Because I associate barbeque with ice cream. I told you earlier about my fiercest barbeque competitor, Bob, and his wife, Donna. After barbeque turn-ins at contests, Donna would walk around and pass out Klondike bars. It always hit the spot. That memory stuck with me, and I wanted to share the emotion of feeling satisfied after a tough long cook.

Now, I'd heard from plenty of people I respect that scaling barbeque is tough—some even said it was impossible without diluting the quality. That was a big fear of mine. So, I figured if I could make the best-tasting ice cream in town, people would come for that and the barbeque—even if the barbeque wasn't as stellar as what we served up north.

At first, it was a grind. The Lone Tree location had worse visibility and parking than our Westminster spot. I had no money for advertising, but I had something more valuable than

an advertising budget. I had an unwavering commitment to giving folks their best twenty minutes of the day. Our guests would come in, have an incredible experience, and they'd leave and spread the word. Slowly but surely, we built the awareness we needed. And eventually, we exceeded our expectations for the Lone Tree shop.

That success gave me the confidence I needed to scale G-Que Barbeque even further, opening a location in Lakewood, followed by three locations inside Empower Field, two inside Folsom Field, and one in Coors Field. And we're not stopping there. By the time this book comes out, we'll have a new location in Thornton and another one in Timnath.

What started as a bare-bones operation has now grown into something bigger than I could have imagined. But here's the truth—growth didn't happen by accident. It happened because we focused on getting better every single day. It's not linear, you take the bad moments and learn from them and don't get complacent or comfortable when things are going well. And that's the key. It's not about waiting for the perfect moment or hoping things will get easier. Take action!

IT'S ABOUT MORE THAN BARBEQUE

When I first started this journey, I thought my goal was to make great barbeque. And while that was the surface-level goal, what I learned about myself along the way was that at my core, I enjoy making people happy. There's nothing better than watching someone take a bite of something you've created and seeing the natural reaction of joy on their face. But as the years went on, I realized there was something else that fueled me—something bigger.

What really drives me isn't just making great barbeque—its helping people realize their own potential. Whether it's a member of my team, a friend, or even a guest, seeing someone recognize what they're capable of and then helping them act on that potential—that's what fulfills me.

At G-Que, we've created a culture that's not just about serving food—it's about serving people. It's about creating an environment where everyone, from the kitchen to the dining room, believes they can achieve something greater than they thought possible. And when someone on my team feels that spark, when they start to see their own value, their own strength—that's the real reward.

Helping people believe in themselves is just as important as any dish we serve. And that's the lesson barbeque has taught me. It's not just about getting the food right—it's about getting the people right. When you build a team, a community, a life, on the foundation of self-belief and a commitment to growth, the results go far beyond barbeque.

Success, I've learned, isn't just about what you can achieve for yourself. It's about how many people you can lift up along the way. When you help others see what they're truly capable of, you're not just making barbeque—you're building something that lasts. Something that changes lives.

EXPERIENCING CHAMPIONSHIP BARBEQUE AT HOME

One of the greatest joys of my journey is being able to share what I've learned with others. Barbeque has always been more than just food for me—cooking for others is a way to connect, to bring people together, and to create lasting memories. And that's why I created this cookbook—so that you, too, can experience the taste of championship-quality barbeque right in your own home. It's not just about following recipes, it's about creating moments that matter, and bringing that experience into your own kitchen or backyard.

This book isn't just a collection of recipes—it's a culmination of years of practice, countless hours spent perfecting techniques, and the valuable lessons I've learned through successes and failures along the way.

Inside, you'll find some of my family's favorite recipes, as well as dishes that have become staples at G-Que. These recipes are designed for everyone no matter where you are on your barbeque journey—whether you're gearing up for a barbeque competition, hosting a weekend cookout, or simply looking to make something special for your loved ones. It doesn't matter if you're a seasoned pitmaster or someone just starting out; the recipes in this book are crafted to bring out the best in your barbeque, one delicious bite at a time.

And for those of you who are eager for more, I've got you covered. Visit my YouTube channel, *G-Que Barbeque*, where I've shared video tutorials that walk you through the process step-by-step. Sometimes, seeing the techniques in action can take your barbeque game to a whole new level. Whether you're looking to fine-tune your brisket or perfect your ribs, the video content is there to give you that extra boost of confidence. I'm here to help you get it right, and, most importantly, remember to enjoy the process.

I consider myself truly blessed to have accomplished all that I have, but I've come to realize that none of it would mean as much if I couldn't share what I've learned with others. It's about more than just sharing recipes—it's about passing on the knowledge, the tips, and the passion for barbeque so that you can create your own magic at home.

So, take these recipes, make them your own by tweaking as you see fit and enjoy them with your friends and family. Because at the end of the day—it's about the people you share life with, the memories you make together, and the joy that comes from gathering around the table with those who matter most.

To everyone who has ever dined at G-Que, told someone about us, or been a part of the G-Que Team—thank you. From the bottom of my heart, I am deeply grateful for each and every one of you. Your support, your belief in what we do, and your contributions have made this journey possible. You are the heartbeat of G-Que.

CHAMPIONSHIP BARBEQUE BEGINS WITH THE PIT

GRILLS AND SMOKERS

In the world of barbeque, the equipment you choose can significantly impact your cooking experience. With a variety of grills and smokers available, each offering unique features, benefits, and challenges, it's important to understand the differences to make an informed decision. This guide will provide an in-depth look at the different types of grills and smokers, their pros and cons, and a comparative analysis to help you choose the right equipment for your barbeque needs.

CHARCOAL GRILLS

Charcoal grills are among the most popular of traditional types of grills. They use charcoal briquettes or lump charcoal as the primary fuel source. Charcoal briquettes are made from a mixture of ground charcoal, coal dust, and other additives that help them bind together and burn more consistently. These ingredients are compressed into uniform shapes, typically small pillow-like pieces. Lump charcoal is made by burning hardwood in a low-oxygen environment until all the natural chemicals, moisture, and sap are removed, leaving behind pure carbon in the shape of irregular, lightweight pieces of charred wood. Lump charcoal is perfect for those who prioritize natural flavor and high heat, while charcoal briquettes offer consistency, longer burn times, and cost efficiency. I think everyone needs a good reliable charcoal grill. Several of my videos on YouTube show you how to smoke on a charcoal grill. If I was told I could only own one grill, this is what I would get. It can't be beat for the price, and you can both grill and smoke on it and produce amazing tasting food.

Pros: Charcoal grills provide a distinctive smoky flavor that is highly prized in barbeque. They are capable of reaching high temperatures, perfect for searing meats. And they are versatile, being suitable for both direct and indirect cooking.

Cons: On the other hand, charcoal grills take longer to heat up and require more effort to maintain the fire. It takes some practice to master temperature control through vents and charcoal arrangement. And they produce more ash, needing to be cleaned out after each use.

Charcoal grills are ideal for traditional barbeque enthusiasts who appreciate the authentic smoky flavor and are willing to invest time in mastering the grill.

GAS GRILLS

Gas grills use propane or natural gas as a fuel source, providing a convenient and efficient grilling option. Natural gas is a fossil fuel composed primarily of methane (CH_4), along with small amounts of other hydrocarbons such as ethane, propane, butane, and pentane. It is extracted from underground reservoirs, often found in conjunction with oil deposits. Once extracted, natural gas undergoes processing to remove impurities and separate other hydrocarbons, resulting in a clean-burning fuel suitable for residential, commercial, and industrial use. Natural gas is a highly efficient, cost-effective, and convenient cooking fuel widely used in residential and commercial settings. Its advantages include consistent heat, precise temperature control, and cleaner burning compared to other fossil fuels. Propane is a hydrocarbon (C_3H_8) that is part of the liquefied petroleum gas (LPG) family. It is a byproduct of natural gas processing and petroleum refining. Propane is stored as a liquid under pressure and vaporizes into a gas when released, making it a versatile and portable fuel source. These are commonly found in the backyards of folks and are suitable for those who want something fast and easy to operate. Since you're reading this book, I assume you're looking to graduate more into the world of smoking, so I would look at an offset or pellet smoker. These are nice to have as a second or third grill.

Pros: Gas grills are quick to heat up and easy to use, making them ideal for everyday grilling. They also offer precise temperature control with adjustable burners. And cleanup is much easier because gas produces less residue.

Cons: Unfortunately, gas grills lack the smoky flavor provided by charcoal or wood. They are also typically more expensive upfront and require a continuous supply of propane or natural gas. Due to the need for a gas supply, they are less portable compared to charcoal grills.

Gas grills are ideal for busy individuals or families looking for a quick and convenient grilling solution without sacrificing performance.

ELECTRIC GRILLS

Electric grills use electricity as their heat source, making them suitable for indoor and outdoor use. You don't see these being used that often, and unless where you live does not allow you to use a non-electric grill, I wouldn't recommend one of these.

Pros: Despite my not being a fan of electric grills, there are some advantages to them. They are extremely user-friendly with simple plug-and-play operation. Since they can be used indoors, they would be great for apartment dwellers. And they offer precise temperature control.

Cons: Of course, electric grills do not provide the smoky flavor of charcoal or wood grills, and they also generally cannot reach the same high temperatures. You are also dependent on having access to an electrical outlet, limiting portability.

Like I've said, electric grills are perfect for those living in apartments or areas with restrictions on open flames who still want to enjoy grilling.

PELLET GRILLS

Pellet grills use compressed wood pellets as fuel, providing a combination of smoking and grilling capabilities with automated temperature control. These pellets are made from sawdust and wood scraps, compressed into small, uniform pieces. The grills and smokers are equipped with a hopper to hold the pellets and an auger system that feeds them into a firebox where they are ignited. This process produces heat and smoke, which cook and flavor the food. These are excellent entry level backyard smokers particularly for those that don't want to have to manage a fire. I used a pellet smoker when I competed and kicked everyone's butt with it, so if anyone tells you that you can't cook good food on a pellet smoker that's simply not true.

Pros: Pellet grills provide a smoky flavor similar to wood or charcoal grills, as well as automated temperature control with digital settings. They are extremely versatile, as you can smoke, grill, bake, roast, and more on them.

Cons: Pellet grills are generally more expensive up front and require a supply of wood pellets. They also require an electrical outlet for operation. More components need to be maintained compared to traditional grills.

Pellet grills are great for barbeque enthusiasts who want the flavor of wood smoking combined with the convenience of automated temperature control.

KAMADO GRILLS

Kamado grills are made from ceramic and are known for their excellent heat retention and versatility. They can be used for grilling, smoking, and baking. Kamado grills are traditionally egg-shaped grills that excel in temperature control. The design is based on ancient Japanese and Chinese clay cooking vessels used for over 3,000 years. Modern kamado grills are made from high-quality ceramic or other advanced heat-retaining materials and are designed to function as versatile outdoor cookers. These are most common in the backyards of folks who want to spend a little more on a backyard cooker. They are great also for cooking steaks and grilling with high heat.

Pros: The kamado grill's excellent heat retention is suited for long, slow cooks. And it can be used for a variety of cooking methods, including grilling, smoking, and baking. Plus, it's made to last.

Cons: Kamado grills are heavy and less portable compared to other grills. And if the ceramic breaks, your pit is shot. Generally, they're more expensive than standard charcoal or gas grills. It also requires some practice to master temperature control.

Kamado grills are made for serious barbeque enthusiasts who want a versatile and durable grill for a variety of cooking methods.

OFFSET SMOKERS

Offset smokers, also known as barrel smokers, have a separate firebox attached to the cooking chamber. The smoke and heat flow from the firebox through the cooking chamber and out a chimney. Offset smokers are a staple in the world of barbeque. They are beloved by pitmasters and barbeque enthusiasts for their ability to produce authentic, rich smoky flavors. Offset smokers offer a traditional approach to smoking meat, allowing for precise control over temperature and smoke levels. This is the most common smoker—you will see them all throughout Texas. Most barbeque restaurants use giant 1,000-gallon offset smokers. And no wonder, these are the best looking of all the barbeque pits out there.

Pros: You'll definitely get that authentic, smoky flavor with an offset smoker. And you can use them for both smoking and grilling. Plus, the large cooking area is suitable for smoking multiple, large cuts of meat.

Cons: Offset smokers usually present a learning curve for beginners—they require frequent monitoring and adjustment to maintain consistent temperature. And they require significant outdoor space.

Offset smokers are great for traditionalists who value authentic smoke flavor and have the space and patience to manage a large smoker.

VERTICAL SMOKERS

Vertical smokers come in two basic styles. Drum smokers are DIY-style smokers made from 55-gallon steel drums. They are simple, efficient, and popular among barbeque enthusiasts for their ability to produce excellent smoked meats. Bullet smokers, sometimes with a water pan, are compact, cylindrical smokers with a distinct bullet shape. They are typically fueled by charcoal and are known for their ease of use and consistent results. I have several YouTube videos where I use a drum smoker, and I am a big fan of them as they produce great results and cook slightly faster than the other cookers mentioned. A drum smoker would be a great first smoker.

Pros: Vertical smokers maximize cooking space with their vertical design. The water pan helps maintain moisture. They are generally easier to use than offset smokers.

Cons: For beginners, maintaining even heat distribution can be challenging. Accessing food on the lower racks can also be cumbersome. The smaller capacity may not accommodate large cuts of meat as easily as other cookers.

Give vertical smokers a try if you're looking for a space-efficient smoker that provides consistent results.

COMPARISON OF GRILLS AND SMOKERS

Flavor: Coming in first place, charcoal and wood grills provide the best smoky flavor. Offset and vertical smokers also offer authentic smoke flavor while giving you the most control. Pellet grills combine convenience with good smoky flavor. And gas and electric grills may offer convenience but lack smoky flavor.

Ease of Use: Electric and gas grills are the most user-friendly with easy temperature control. Pellet grills are also onvenient with automated controls but require electricity. Charcoal grills demand more effort to manage temperature and fire. Offset and vertical smokers need frequent monitoring and adjustment.

Versatility: Kamado, charcoal, and pellet grills are all extremely versatile, being suitable for grilling, smoking, baking, and more. Offset and vertical smokers, as the name implies, are best for smoking but can be used for grilling with adjustments. On the other hand, gas and electric grills are made for grilling and are less suitable for smoking.

Cost: Charcoal and gas grills are generally affordable with options at various price points. Electric grills are moderately priced, depending on features. Pellet grills and kamado grills present a higher up-front cost with ongoing fuel expenses. However, entry level models of these last two can be reasonable, but you do get what you pay for in terms of insulation and even cooking. And finally, offset and vertical smokers vary widely in price based on size and features.

Choosing the right grill or smoker depends on your specific needs, preferences, and cooking style. By understanding the pros and cons of each type of grill and smoker, you can make an informed decision and elevate your barbeque skills to the next level. One of the most common questions I get is what kind of pit I should buy. My recommendation would be to go into a local barbeque supply shop and talk with them. Most large cities have boutique barbeque supply shops with passionate, knowledgeable folks that love talking barbeque and will want to find the right pit for you. Here in Denver, we have Proud Souls Barbecue and a place like that is where I would go first.

WOODS, COALS, AND FUELS

The choice of fuel for smoking and grilling is an important decision. Think of it as an ingredient to cooking just like you would a rub or sauce recipe. You want your fuel to complement the protein you're preparing. My opinion is that the smoke or grill flavor shouldn't overpower the protein. For instance, if you're cooking brisket, you should taste beef first. If you're grilling a fish, fish should be the prevailing taste, not smoke. Various fuels can be used, each offering unique characteristics and advantages. This guide will provide an overview of the different types of fuels used for smoking and grilling, compare them, and conclude with key takeaways.

TYPES OF FUELS

Lump Charcoal

Lump charcoal is made from pure hardwood, charred in an oxygen-limited environment.

It comes in irregular shapes and sizes and has a lot going for it—it burns hotter and faster than briquettes; produces a natural, smoky flavor; and contains no additives or chemicals. On the other hand, because of its irregular shape, it burns unevenly, and its shorter burn time requires more frequent refueling. It's also more expensive than briquettes.

Charcoal Briquettes

Charcoal briquettes are made from compressed charcoal, along with binders and additives, resulting in a uniform shape and size. As far as its benefits, it burns longer and more consistently than lump charcoal, is easier to stack and arrange for heat, and is generally more affordable. Unfortunately, its additives and fillers can affect flavor. It produces more ash, requiring more cleanup. It also has a lower maximum temperature compared to lump charcoal.

Wood

Wood fuel is available as logs, chunks, chips, or pellets. As you might imagine, different types of wood impart different flavors and some popular kinds include hickory, mesquite, and applewood. Wood fuel provides the most authentic smoky flavor and can be used for both high-heat grilling and low-and-slow smoking. Of course, using wood requires more skill to manage and maintain the fire. And it also produces more smoke, which can be a nuisance in certain settings. Plus, you'll need to have more space to store logs and chunks of wood.

TYPES OF WOOD FOR COOKING

The type of wood used in smoking and grilling significantly influences the flavor of the food. Each wood variety imparts its own unique aroma and taste, enhancing the overall culinary experience. This guide will compare and contrast different types of wood commonly used for cooking, discussing their characteristics, ideal uses, and how they differ from one another.

Apple

Applewood's mild, sweet and fruity flavor is best for pork, poultry and fish. Its delicate sweetness is suitable for a wide range of meats and vegetables, as it enhances the natural flavors of the meat. But since it burns at a lower temperature, it requires longer cooking times. And it may be too mild for those who prefer a stronger smoke flavor.

Cherry

Cherry is another sweet, mild, and fruity wood ideal for pork, poultry, beef, and lamb. It adds both a subtle, sweet flavor, without overpowering the meat, and a beautiful mahogany color to the food. Of course, this mild flavor may not be noticeable with heavily seasoned meats. And keep in mind that it burns slightly faster than some other hardwoods.

Hickory

Hickory imparts a strong, smoky, and bacon-like flavor, and pairs well with rich meats like pork, ribs, ham, bacon, and sausages. It is versatile and commonly available.

Mesquite

Mesquite offers an intense, earthy, and slightly sweet flavor, which is best for beef, brisket, and wild game. Its bold, distinctive flavor may be too strong for delicate meats and vegetables. It burns hot and fast, making it ideal for quick grilling. But watch out—it can easily become overpowering or bitter.

Oak

Oak's balanced smoke flavor complements a variety of meats, including beef, lamb, pork, and fish. It burns slowly and evenly, making it ideal for long smoking sessions. However, its flavor may be too mild for those seeking a strong smoky taste, and its availability varies by region.

Pecan

The rich, nutty, and sweet taste of pecan wood adds a complex flavor that enhances the taste of many meats, including pork, poultry, fish, and beef. The flavor just won't be as pronounced as hickory or mesquite. Since it burns cooler than other woods, pecan is suitable for low and slow cooking but requires careful heat management. It can also be more expensive than other woods.

COMPARING DIFFERENT WOOD FUELS

Flavor Profile: Hickory and mesquite provide intense, robust flavors suitable for rich meats like pork and beef. Applewood and cherrywood, meanwhile, offer mild, sweet flavors ideal for poultry, fish, and pork. Oak and pecan provide a medium smoke flavor, making them versatile for a wide range of meats.

Burn Rate and Temperature: Mesquite burns quickly and at high temperatures, ideal for searing. Oak and pecan burn slowly and evenly, perfect for long smoking sessions. Hickory and maple burn at a moderate rate, suitable for most smoking and grilling needs. Alder burns cooler and faster, making it best for short smoking times.

Ideal Uses: Hickory and mesquite are best for beef, pork, and game due to their strong flavors. Applewood, cherrywood, alder, and maple are ideal for delicate meats like fish, poultry, and pork, providing subtle, sweet smoke. Oak and pecan are suitable for a wide range of meats, offering a balanced flavor and slow burn.

Have fun using different wood fuels and don't get too stressed out about picking the wrong type. I would say you need to use mesquite with caution as it's so strong. Otherwise play around with different flavors to see what you like best. When competing I used 80% hickory and 20%

cherry. In the restaurants we use 100% hickory mostly driven by cost and availability. I love a little bit of cherry, and I think it provides nice color to the meat also. By understanding the characteristics and best uses of each type of wood, you can enhance your barbeque experience and achieve the perfect smoky flavor for any dish.

COMPARING OTHER FUELS

Propane: Propane gas is portable and convenient for outdoor cooking with your gas grill or smoker. It provides consistent heat, is easy to control and quick to start up and heat up. Of course, it lacks the smoky flavor of charcoal or wood. And you'll have to regularly refill your tanks, making for higher operating costs compared to charcoal.

Natural Gas: Natural gas is similar to propane but delivered via a pipeline in your home directly to the grill. That means you'll never run out of fuel as long as the supply is connected. And it's more cost effective over time compared to propane. It also provides consistent, controllable heat. But the initial installation can be expensive, and it's less portable since it's fixed to a specific location. Also, like propane, it lacks a smoky flavor.

Pellets: Pellets are made from compressed sawdust and wood scraps and are used in pellet grills and smokers. They offer precise temperature control with digital settings, providing a consistent, long-lasting burn. You'll need an electricity source to operate the auger and control systems. Various wood types offer different flavors, albeit less smoky than traditional wood. Generally, pellets are more expensive up front, and you'll have to restock your pellets on an ongoing basis.

Electric: Using electricity to generate heat means you can grill both indoors and out, making it suitable for areas with restrictions on open flames. Electric grills are extremely easy to use with plug and play operation and consistent temperature control. Unfortunately, you'll miss the smoky flavor from charcoal, wood, or pellets and you can only grill where you have access to electricity.

VARIOUS WOOD TYPES OFFER DIFFERENT FLAVORS, ALBEIT LESS SMOKY THAN TRADITIONAL WOOD.

COMPARISON OF FUELS

Choosing the right fuel for smoking and grilling depends on your specific needs, preferences, and cooking style. Charcoal (both lump and briquettes) offers a traditional smoky flavor and high heat, making it ideal for authentic barbeque experiences. Wood provides the richest smoky flavors but requires more skill and attention. Propane and natural gas offer convenience and precise temperature control but lack the depth of flavor from charcoal and wood. Pellets combine convenience with a mild smoky flavor, making them suitable for a variety of cooking methods. Electric grills are perfect for indoor use and areas with restrictions on open flames but lack the classic smoky flavor. By understanding the characteristics, pros, and cons of each fuel type, you can make an informed decision that enhances your grilling and smoking experience, ensuring delicious and flavorful results every time.

COMPARISON OF FUELS	FLAVOR	HEAT CONTROL	CONVENIENCE	COST	BEST FOR
LUMP CHARCOAL	NATURAL, SMOKY	MODERATE, RESPONSIVE	MODERATE	MODERATE-HIGH	HIGH-HEAT GRILLING, SMOKY FLAVOR
CHARCOAL BRIQUETTES	MILD, CONSISTENT	MODERATE, CONSISTENT	MODERATE	LOW-MODERATE	LONG SMOKING SESSIONS, AFFORDABILITY
WOOD	RICH, AUTHENTIC	LOW, MANUAL	LOW	VARIABLE	AUTHENTIC BARBEQUE, VARIETY OF FLAVORS
PROPANE	NEUTRAL	HIGH, PRECISE	HIGH	MODERATE	CONVENIENCE, CONSISTENT GRILLING
NATURAL GAS	NEUTRAL	HIGH, PRECISE	HIGH	LOW-MODERATE	CONTINUOUS FUEL SUPPLY, CONVENIENCE
PELLETS	MILD, SMOKY	HIGH, AUTOMATED	HIGH	HIGH	SET-IT-AND-FORGET-IT COOKING
ELECTRIC	NEUTRAL	HIGH, AUTOMATED	HIGH	LOW-MODERATE	INDOOR USE, EASE OF USE

BASICS TO MANAGING FIRE AND SMOKE

Grilling and smoking are versatile cooking methods that can be divided into two primary techniques: direct and indirect cooking. Each method offers unique advantages and is suited for different types of meats and cooking goals. Understanding the differences between direct and indirect cooking will help you choose the best approach for your barbeque needs, ensuring delicious and perfectly cooked results every time.

Before we discuss direct and indirect heating, it's important that we break in our new smoker so we can achieve the two methods of cooking I'm about to describe.

BREAK IN THE SMOKER USING THE BISCUIT TEST

When you're breaking in a brand-new smoker, the first thing to learn is how it cooks. Every smoker has its own quirks and unique temperature patterns or hotspots, and to get the best results, a pitmaster must know how to work with them. That's where the "biscuit test" comes in. This technique is a simple, reliable way to map out the hot and cool zones inside a smoker. By placing uncooked biscuits across the grates, you can see exactly how heat is distributed, as each biscuit browns at a different rate depending on the intensity of the heat in its spot. A quicker browning or even burning shows where heat accumulates, while slower, pale biscuits reveal cooler zones.

The biscuit test serves a dual purpose for pitmasters: it's a practical approach to understanding your smoker's "personality," and it's a way to save time, effort, and mistakes down the line. If you dive right into smoking meat without testing, you risk cooking inconsistently, with some cuts overcooking or undercooking due to uneven heat recognition. With the biscuit test, you gain valuable insight into how to best arrange food, making it easier to avoid those rookie mistakes. It's a chance to refine your technique and work with, rather than against, the smoker's natural heat distribution. You will learn where the hotspots are so you can place the larger part of the protein in or toward the hotspot.

Mastering the biscuit test is about more than just finding hot spots; it's a reminder of the importance of understanding your equipment intimately. To be the best pitmaster, you must treat each smoker as its own tool, learning its strengths and challenges. Once you've pinpointed these heat zones, you can adapt your smoking strategy with confidence, knowing exactly how to place, rotate, and manage your food for consistent, even cooking results. Add some jelly, butter, or honey to the biscuits for a little pitmaster privilege after your test.

DIRECT COOKING

Direct cooking involves placing the food directly over the heat source. This method is commonly used for grilling, where the heat from charcoal, gas, or electric elements cooks the food quickly, typically a few minutes per side. Temperatures can usually reach up to 450°F to 700°F (232°C to 371°C). The high heat caramelizes the surface of the meat, adding depth to the flavor. Of course, with this high heat, there is the risk of overcooking or burning food if not monitored closely.

Direct cooking is ideal for foods that cook quickly, such as steaks, burgers, hot dogs, chicken breasts, vegetables, and seafood. The searing that occurs creates a delicious crust and char marks, enhancing the flavor and texture. I would only use direct cooking for small cuts of meat, as it is not suitable for large cuts that require longer cooking times.

INDIRECT COOKING

Indirect cooking involves placing the food away from the heat source, creating a gentler and more even cooking environment. The food is placed on the grill grates away from the heat source, with the heat circulating around the food. This method is often used for smoking and slow cooking, with longer cooking times ranging from one hour to several hours. And the temperatures are lower, typically between 225°F to 350°F (107°C to 177°C).

Indirect cooking provides a more uniform heat, reducing the risk of burning or overcooking. It's ideal for large cuts of meat that require slow cooking to break down connective tissues, resulting in tender and juicy meat. And it allows for the infusion of smoky flavors over a longer period, enhancing the depth of flavor. Those longer cooking times require patience and planning. And you may need more space on the grill to position food away from the heat source. Indirect cooking is best for brisket, ribs, whole chickens and turkeys, pork shoulders, roasts, and large fish.

Both direct and indirect cooking methods offer unique benefits and are suited for different types of meats and cooking goals. Direct cooking is ideal for quick, high heat grilling tasks, delivering deliciously seared and charred results. Indirect cooking excels at low-and-slow smoking and roasting, producing tender, flavorful meats that benefit from extended cooking times. By understanding the strengths and appropriate uses of each method, you can improve your barbeque skills and consistently achieve mouthwatering results, whether you're grilling a steak or smoking a brisket.

The absolute best way to set up your grill with charcoal and wood is a method called two-zone cooking. I will refer to it often through the recipes.

TWO-ZONE COOKING

Two-zone cooking is a versatile and effective grilling technique that provides greater control over cooking temperatures, allowing for both direct and indirect cooking on the same grill. This method is particularly useful for achieving perfectly cooked meats and vegetables, ensuring that food is neither overcooked nor undercooked. This guide will explain what two-zone cooking is, what it is used for, how to set it up, and the benefits it offers.

Two-zone cooking involves creating two distinct heat zones on a grill: a high-heat, direct cooking zone and a low-heat, indirect cooking zone. This setup allows for greater flexibility and precision in cooking, making it possible to sear and then slowly cook food to the desired doneness.

USES OF TWO-ZONE COOKING

Searing and Finishing: Perfect for meats that benefit from a quick sear over high heat, followed by gentle cooking to reach the desired internal temperature.

DIRECT

DIRECT

INDIRECT

Cooking Different Foods Simultaneously: Allows for cooking foods with different temperature requirements at the same time (e.g., grilling vegetables on low heat while searing steaks on high heat).

Reverse Searing: Ideal for the reverse sear technique, where food is first cooked indirectly at a low temperature and then seared at high heat for a flavorful crust.

Managing Flare-Ups: Provides a safe zone to move food if flare-ups occur, reducing the risk of burning.

HOW TO SET UP TWO-ZONE COOKING

Charcoal Grills

Light a sufficient amount of charcoal using a chimney starter or lighter cubes. Once the charcoal is ashed over, push the coals over to one side (direct zone) and leave the other side with no coals (indirect zone). Place a drip pan filled with water or other liquids beneath the indirect cooking zone to catch drippings and help regulate temperature. Open the vents fully for high heat on the direct side and partially on the indirect side to control airflow and temperature.

Gas Grills

Turn all burners on high and preheat the grill with the lid closed. Then turn off one or more burners to create the indirect zone. Leave one or more burners on high for the direct zone. Place food over the lit burners for direct cooking and move it to the unlit side for indirect cooking. Use built-in thermometers or an external grill thermometer to monitor and maintain desired temperatures in each zone.

BENEFITS OF TWO-ZONE COOKING

With two-zone cooking, you can better control your cooking temperatures, reducing the risk of overcooking or undercooking. This allows you to achieve a perfect sear while ensuring the interior is cooked to the desired doneness, resulting in juicier and more flavorful food. You can avoid uneven cooking by allowing for a gentler heat application on the indirect side.

HOW TO APPLY TWO-ZONE COOKING

Steaks and Burgers

Sear steaks or burgers on the direct heat side to develop a crust, then move them to the indirect side to finish cooking to the desired internal temperature without burning.

Whole Chickens

Place the whole chicken on the indirect side to cook slowly and evenly, then move to the direct side for a final sear to crisp up the skin.

Vegetables

Grill vegetables on the indirect side while cooking meats on the direct side, ensuring both are done at the same time without overcooking the vegetables.

Two-zone cooking is a powerful technique that enhances the versatility and precision of grilling. By creating distinct direct and indirect heat zones, you can achieve perfect sears, manage flare-ups, and cook different types of food simultaneously. It allows you to be in complete control of your barbeque and is my go to method when on the grill.

MUST-HAVE TOOLS AND EQUIPMENT

Grilling and smoking are culinary arts that benefit from the right tools and gadgets. These essential items can enhance your cooking experience, improve safety, and help you achieve consistently delicious results. This guide will outline the must-have gadgets for grilling and smoking, explaining why they are important, and how they contribute to successful barbeque sessions. I will rank them from most important to least important.

Whether you're a novice or a seasoned pitmaster, having items like an instant-read thermometer, long-handled tongs, heat-resistant gloves, and a chimney starter can make a substantial difference in your cooking. By investing in these must-have gadgets, you'll be well-prepared to tackle any grilling or smoking challenge and elevate your barbeque skills.

INSTANT-READ THERMOMETER

You can't manage what you can't measure. Be sure to spend the extra money for the instant read as it gives you an accurate reading right away which is important when grilling.

Precision Cooking: Ensures that meat reaches the correct internal temperature, preventing undercooking or overcooking.

Safety: Reduces the risk of foodborne illnesses by confirming that meats are cooked to safe temperatures.

Consistency: Helps achieve the desired doneness every time, whether you're grilling steak or smoking a turkey.

HEAT-RESISTANT GLOVES AND NITRILE GLOVES

I like to put a pair of nitrile gloves over heat-resistant gloves to keep them clean and protect them from wear and tear.

Protection: Protects your hands and arms from burns when handling hot grill grates, coals, and cooking utensils.

Flexibility: Allows for better maneuverability and grip compared to using towels or mitts.

Safety: Essential for tasks like adding fuel, adjusting vents, or moving hot items.

JAVELIN
-40 / +482°F / +250°C
170.4 °F

CLEAN THOSE GRATES

It's important before you grill to make sure your grates are clean. I recommend heating the grill to as hot as possible to burn off any prior grease or residue. If there's a lot of charred bits still stuck on the grates, use a ball of aluminum foil to scrape it off. Then take some paper towels dipped in oil (or used an oiled towel) and rub the grates back and forth. The goal is to have clean grill grates, so your food tastes like food and not burnt char from a dirty grill. The best time to clean the grates is right after you cook. It's much easier to clean when everything is hot.

ALUMINUM FOIL

Sure, you can spend your money on a fancy wire brush and have one of the needles break off into your food or just get a wad of foil and use it to keep your grill grates clean.

Cleanliness: Essential for maintaining a clean cooking surface by removing stuck-on food and grease.

Health: Prevents old food particles and residues from contaminating fresh food.

Efficiency: Ensures even heat distribution by keeping grill grates free from buildup.

CHIMNEY STARTER

If you've ever seen me cook, you know I like to use chimney starters to get the fire started.

Efficiency: Quickly and evenly lights charcoal without the need for lighter fluid, which can impart unwanted flavors.

Environmentally Friendly: Uses natural fire starters, reducing chemical use.

Consistency: Ensures an even and reliable start to your charcoal grilling session.

MEAT PROBES AND WIRELESS THERMOMETERS

Spend more time with your family and friends instead of hovering over a pit taking temperature readings.

Remote Monitoring: Allows you to monitor the internal temperature of your meat from a distance, reducing the need to open the grill or smoker.

Accuracy: Provides real-time updates and alarms, helping you maintain consistent cooking temperatures.

Convenience: Many models come with smartphone apps for easy monitoring and control.

LONG-HANDLED TONGS

Safety: Keeps your hands at a safe distance from high heat and flames.

Control: Provides a firm grip on food, making it easier to turn and move items on the grill without piercing them and losing juices.

Versatility: Ideal for flipping steaks, moving vegetables, and handling larger cuts of meat.

OTHER PIT FUNDAMENTALS

SELECTING THE BEST MEATS FOR BARBEQUE

Choosing the right meat is one of the most critical steps in creating mouthwatering barbeque. The quality and characteristics of the meat form the foundation of the entire cooking process, so this is not an area where you want to cut corners. Whether you're selecting beef, pork, or seafood, paying attention to details like marbling, fat content, color, and the freshness of the product can make all the difference. After years of trial and error in both competitions and my restaurants, I've learned a few key principles that guide my meat selection, which I'm excited to share with you.

The USDA grading system for beef is a great starting point, but it's only part of the equation. Similarly, picking the perfect rack of pork ribs goes beyond just grabbing whatever looks the biggest or most meaty. Each cut has unique qualities that determine how well it will stand up to the long, slow cooking process essential to true barbeque. The idea is to select cuts that allow you to take full advantage of their natural fat content and structure, turning every ounce of connective tissue into melt-in-your-mouth deliciousness.

Then there's seafood. While it may seem like a wildcard for barbeque purists, seafood can hold its own on the smoker or grill. But again, the freshness and fat content will make or break the dish. Whether you're grilling fish filets or smoking a whole side of salmon, knowing how to choose seafood that retains moisture and absorbs flavor is crucial. Let's break this down, starting with the king of all barbeque meats—beef.

Beef: Wagyu, Prime, and Choice

There's a reason barbeque competitions and high-end restaurants emphasize the importance of beef grading. Beef quality, particularly when it comes to marbling—the white flecks of fat within the muscle, directly impacts how the meat behaves on the smoker. When you're selecting beef for barbeque, the goal is to pick cuts that have enough marbling to stay tender and juicy through long cooks, while also delivering the rich, beefy flavor that's synonymous with great barbeque.

Wagyu Beef

Wagyu, especially Japanese Wagyu, is in a class of its own. The extreme marbling in Wagyu creates a buttery texture that almost melts in your mouth. This high level of intramuscular fat ensures that even the leaner parts of the meat stay moist during cooking. What sets Wagyu apart is not just the amount of marbling, but the quality of the fat. Wagyu fat has a lower melting point than regular beef, so it begins to render almost immediately, basting the meat from the inside out as it cooks.

This makes Wagyu perfect for cuts like brisket or roasts, where long cooking times are necessary. You end up with an incredibly rich, decadent piece of meat that offers a flavor and texture profile you simply can't get with other grades. For competition-level barbeque, Wagyu is a game-changer. It's what all the top-level brisket cooks use when competing. When I want to create a truly memorable experience—something that will make people stop and savor every bite—I reach for Wagyu.

However, Wagyu's richness can be overwhelming in large quantities, so I like to balance it by serving it alongside other cuts or complementing it with bright, acidic sauces that cut through the fat. Wagyu is also best cooked with minimal seasoning, as the natural flavor of the beef shines without much need for enhancement. A simple salt and pepper rub often does the trick, letting the meat speak for itself.

Prime Beef

Prime beef is the highest USDA grade and is the sweet spot for most barbeque enthusiasts. It has ample marbling, which helps keep the meat juicy during the long, slow smoking process, but it's not as intensely fatty as Wagyu, making it a bit more versatile and less rich. Prime beef offers that balance between luxury and accessibility. Whether it's a brisket, ribeye, or short rib, prime-grade beef delivers excellent results on the smoker or grill.

For brisket in particular, prime beef is ideal. Brisket is notorious for being a tough cut because it comes from a part of the cow that does a lot of work, but prime brisket has just the right amount of marbling to break down and render during the cook, leaving you with tender, flavorful slices. The fat cap on a prime brisket, which you want to leave intact, helps the meat retain moisture and protects it from drying out while it cooks. Over the hours of smoking, that fat renders beautifully into the meat, giving you those signature juicy, melt-in-your-mouth bites. Approximately only the top 5 to 7% of cattle in America grade out at prime depending on the year.

Choice Beef

Choice beef, the second-highest grade in the USDA system, is still an excellent option for barbeque, particularly for home cooks who may not want to splurge on Wagyu or prime for every meal. Choice beef has less marbling than prime, but with the right cut and cooking method, you can still achieve fantastic results.

For example, a choice-grade brisket might require a bit more attention to ensure it stays moist. This is where techniques like injecting, wrapping in butcher paper, or adding extra fat (like bacon or beef tallow) can come into play. You're working with slightly leaner meat, so you need to focus on preserving moisture during the long cook. However, if you hit it right, you can get a brisket from choice beef that's nearly as tender and flavorful as prime.

Every year in America, 50 to 55% of meat gets graded as choice, not prime. If selecting choice, look for those cuts with more striations than those with less. You're paying the same regardless, however the taste and flavor will be noticeably different. Sometimes when looking over the meat at the butcher shop you can even see high end choice that has better marbling than prime cuts.

OTHER FACTORS TO CONSIDER WHEN CHOOSING BEEF

Beyond grade, there are other factors I consider when choosing beef. The breed of the cattle, how it was raised, and its diet all influence the flavor and texture of the meat. Grass-fed beef tends to have a more pronounced beefy flavor, while grain-fed beef has more marbling. I typically prefer grain-fed beef for barbeque because of the higher fat content, but grass-fed can shine in certain preparations if you're looking for a leaner option with a robust flavor.

Additionally, when selecting cuts like brisket, I pay attention to the size and shape. I want a brisket that is thick and uniform across the flat and point, which helps ensure even cooking. Thin or tapered edges on the flat can dry out quickly, so I avoid cuts with those characteristics. The best brisket has a nice fat cap and a deep red color, indicating freshness.

PORK RIBS: AVOIDING SHINERS AND FAT POCKETS

When selecting pork ribs, you have to be equally as discerning. One of the biggest mistakes is picking a rack that looks impressive at first glance but hides flaws that will cause problems during the cook. The ideal rack of ribs will have a consistent layer of meat across the bones and a good balance of fat. You want enough fat to keep the meat moist, but too much fat—especially fat pockets—can lead to uneven cooking and greasiness.

A "shiner" is when the bones of the ribs are exposed, with little to no meat covering them. This happens when the butcher cuts too close to the bone, and while it's not a dealbreaker, it does mean there's less meat on the rack. Avoid racks with a lot of shiners, because the ribs will cook unevenly and won't be as satisfying to eat. The best racks have a uniform thickness of meat from one end to the other, ensuring each bite is tender and juicy.

When shopping for ribs, the meat should feel firm to the touch, not slimy or sticky. Baby back ribs tend to have more tender meat, while spareribs offer a bit more fat and flavor. Both can be fantastic on the smoker, but I lean toward spareribs for that extra richness. Also avoid three-packs when possible as packers like to bury the "bad" racks in the middle. Best to look for single racks so you know exactly what you're getting.

SEAFOOD FOR THE GRILL

Barbeque and grilling isn't just about land-based meats; seafood is an underrated but fantastic option for the smoker or grill. The key to great grilled seafood is selecting fish or shellfish that can handle high heat without falling apart or drying out. I tend to gravitate toward fattier, firm-textured fish like salmon, tuna, or swordfish. The higher fat content helps these types of fish stay moist, even when exposed to the high temperatures of the grill or smoker.

When selecting seafood, freshness is paramount. I look for bright, clear eyes in whole fish, shiny skin, and a clean, briny smell—if it smells "fishy," it's not fresh. For filets, I want a firm texture, no discoloration, and a glossy sheen. Salmon, in particular, should have a vibrant orange color with thick marbling of fat running through the flesh. This fat is essential because it helps the fish stay succulent while it absorbs the smoky flavor.

Shellfish like shrimp or scallops are another great option. I prefer jumbo shrimp for the grill because they're less likely to overcook. They should be firm, with a mild briny scent and translucent flesh. When grilling scallops, I go for the largest, freshest sea scallops I can find, ensuring they have a sweet, oceanic aroma. The high heat caramelizes the outside, creating a perfect contrast to the tender interior.

ESSENTIAL INGREDIENTS FOR THE PANTRY AND REFRIGERATOR

Creating great barbeque requires more than just skill with the grill or smoker—it's about having the right ingredients ready to elevate every cook. Whether you're preparing a dry rub, seasoning meat, or finishing a dish, a well-stocked pantry and refrigerator give you the tools to make every meal memorable. Here are the essential ingredients I believe every home barbeque cook should always have:

PANTRY STAPLES

Kosher Salt

Salt is the backbone of any barbeque, and kosher salt is the go-to for most cooks. Its coarse texture allows for even seasoning and slow absorption into the meat, making it perfect for dry brining or seasoning large cuts like brisket and pork shoulder. The larger crystals are easy to control, ensuring you don't over-salt, and it works well for both prepping and seasoning before the cook.

Sea Salt

Sea salt, with its fine crystals and mild, mineral-rich flavor, is great for seasoning lighter meats and seafood, where you want a subtler touch. It dissolves quickly, making it a fantastic choice for marinades or for seasoning fish and chicken. Sea salt also works well in sauces or when you want to add a little extra flavor after cooking.

Flake Salt

Flake salt, known for its large, crunchy crystals, is ideal for finishing barbequed meats. After you've sliced brisket or pork ribs, a sprinkle of flake salt adds both texture and a final pop of flavor. It's a great way to elevate the presentation and taste of your barbeque, offering that perfect salty bite without overwhelming the dish.

Brown Sugar

Brown sugar is essential for adding sweetness and helping create a caramelized crust (or bark) on smoked meats. The molasses in brown sugar adds complexity, which works especially well on ribs, pork shoulder, and even chicken. It's a must-have when you want to balance sweetness with savory and spicy flavors in your rubs and sauces.

Paprika (Sweet or Smoked)

Paprika brings both color and flavor to your barbeque. Sweet paprika adds a mild peppery warmth, while smoked paprika adds a deeper, smoky flavor that enhances slow-cooked meats. Both types are versatile and essential for rubs and sauces, giving your dishes a rich red color and a subtle earthy note.

Black Pepper

Coarse black pepper is a staple for adding sharpness and bite to your barbeque. It's essential for beef cuts like brisket and short ribs, where its heat cuts through the richness of the meat. Black pepper also contributes to the formation of that perfect crust or bark that every pitmaster strives for.

Garlic Powder and Onion Powder

Garlic powder and onion powder are essential for building depth of flavor in your rubs and marinades. They're especially useful when fresh garlic or onions might burn at high heat. These powders distribute evenly and boost the savory elements of any meat, whether it's pork, chicken, or beef.

Chili Powder

Chili powder adds warmth and earthiness to your rubs, working well on pork and chicken. It's a versatile ingredient that complements the sweetness of brown sugar and the heat of cayenne, making it a great choice for rubs and sauces that need an extra layer of flavor.

Cayenne Pepper

For those who love a bit of heat, cayenne pepper is an essential pantry ingredient. Just a pinch adds a slow-building spiciness to your barbeque, balancing the sweetness from sugars or honey. Cayenne is great for rubs, sauces, or finishing dishes with a touch of heat.

Mustard (Dry and Prepared)

Mustard is a secret weapon for barbequers. Dry mustard powder adds tangy sharpness to rubs, while prepared mustard can be slathered on meat to help the rub adhere and add flavor. It's especially useful on pork and ribs, where the acidity of the mustard cuts through the fat and balances the sweetness of the rub.

Apple Cider Vinegar

Apple cider vinegar is a barbequer's best friend. It's perfect for spritzing meats during the cooking process, keeping them moist and adding a touch of acidity to balance the richness of smoked meats. Apple cider vinegar is also a key ingredient in many barbeque sauces, particularly for pulled pork and ribs, where its tang brightens the flavors.

Honey

Honey is a fantastic sweetener for glazes and sauces, helping create a sticky, caramelized finish on ribs or chicken. Its natural sweetness pairs well with the heat of spices like cayenne or chili powder, creating a balanced flavor profile that complements smoked meats.

Hot Sauce

Every barbequer should have a favorite hot sauce on hand. Whether you're adding a few dashes to marinades, rubs, or sauces, hot sauce brings a kick of heat and tanginess that can enhance any barbeque dish. Louisiana-style hot sauces, with their vinegar base, are especially good for cutting through rich, fatty meats like pork or brisket.

G-Que Barbeque 'The Rub'

While building your own rubs is great, every home barbequer should have a go-to commercial rub ready to use. Recognizing I am biased, I recommend keeping a bottle of G-Que Barbeque's 'The Rub' in your pantry. It's a balanced blend of savory and sweet flavors that works on just about anything—whether you're grilling chicken, smoking ribs, or searing steaks. Having a high-quality commercial rub on hand is convenient and ensures you can always add the perfect layer of flavor to your barbeque, even when you're short on time. I use it in place of anything I use salt and pepper on; it's also great on vegetables or potatoes. We use it at G-Que on every protein and many of the sides, and several other barbeque restaurants also use G-Que's The Rub.

REFRIGERATOR STAPLES

Butter (Unsalted)

Unsalted butter is a fantastic ingredient for basting meats like steak or chicken during grilling, adding a rich, velvety finish. You can also use it in finishing sauces or to brush onto meats right before serving, giving them that extra touch of moisture and flavor.

Fresh Herbs (Thyme, Rosemary, Parsley)

Fresh herbs bring an aromatic quality to barbequed meats. Thyme and rosemary work particularly well with beef and lamb, while parsley adds brightness when sprinkled on finished dishes. Fresh herbs elevate any marinade or rub, providing a fresh, earthy note to complement the smoky flavors of barbeque.

Lemon and Lime

Citrus fruits like lemons and limes are essential for adding brightness to barbeque, especially with lighter meats like chicken or seafood. A squeeze of lemon or lime at the end of cooking cuts through the richness of smoked meats and enhances the overall flavor.

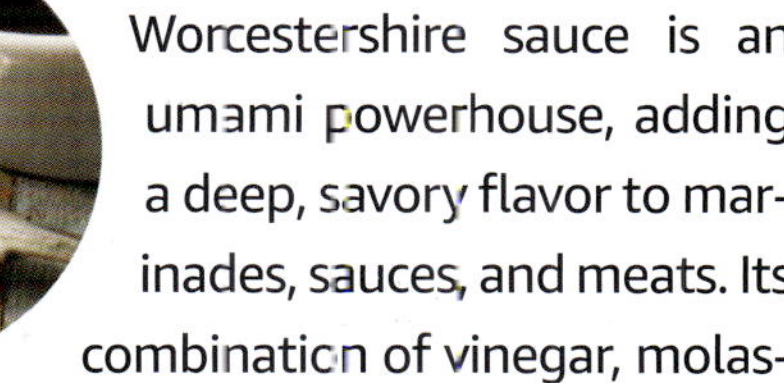

Worcestershire Sauce

Worcestershire sauce is an umami powerhouse, adding a deep, savory flavor to marinades, sauces, and meats. Its combination of vinegar, molasses, and anchovies provides complexity, making it ideal for any pork protein in my opinion.

Beer

Beer is both a barbequer's drink of choice and a versatile ingredient. It's great for adding malty sweetness to marinades, braising liquids, or sauces. If you're having a bad day, it can also make your troubles melt away along with a plate of ribs.

Barbeque Sauce

A solid barbeque sauce is a must-have for finishing ribs, pulled pork, or chicken. Whether homemade or store-bought, having a well-balanced sauce in the fridge that combines sweet, tangy, and spicy elements is the perfect way to finish your barbeque. G-Que Barbeque's signature sauces are great examples of versatile, flavorful sauces that enhances any smoked meat. G-Que's 'Hottish' is my favorite barbeque sauce.

With these essential pantry and refrigerator items, you'll always be prepared to create amazing barbeque. From the right salts and spices to your favorite bottle of rub, these ingredients ensure you can bring out the best in every dish.

THE CLAS

{RECIPES}

SICS

THE MEATS

Classic barbeque meats, when prepared at home, bring a sense of tradition and bold flavors to the table.

Beef brisket is a cornerstone of barbeque and kicks off this chapter. Known for its rich marbling and smoky tenderness after being cooked low and slow, a well-prepared brisket boasts a flavorful bark on the outside, with a juicy, melt-in-your-mouth interior.

Ribs are another classic choice and featured in the pages ahead. Seasoned with a dry rub or marinated, they are typically smoked for hours, allowing the meat to become tender enough to fall off the bone. Whether you prefer a tangy vinegar-based sauce or a sweeter, sticky glaze, ribs are a crowd favorite.

Pulled pork, usually made from the pork shoulder, is cooked over low heat until it's tender enough to shred with a fork. As you'll discover in this chapter, the slow cooking process allows the pork fat to render, leaving the meat juicy and flavorful. It's often served with a smoky or spicy barbeque sauce and piled high on sandwiches or plates.

Finally, we'll wrap up the chapter with classic barbeque sausage. Often smoked or grilled, these tasty links add a spicy and savory element to the barbeque spread. Whether it's a simple pork sausage or a more complex blend, its bold flavors make it a great accompaniment to the other barbeque meats.

BEEF BRISKET

Brisket is a cut of meat that, when prepared correctly, embodies the epitome of barbeque perfection. Its intrinsic mysterious qualities make it one of the most flavorful and satisfying meats to cook and eat. The magic lies in the meat's marbling and connective tissues, which the low and slow cooking process transforms into tender, melt-in-your-mouth goodness. The intramuscular fat slowly renders, infusing the meat with rich, buttery flavors that make every bite a rewarding experience. The natural basting process ensures the brisket remains juicy and succulent throughout the long cooking period.

The smoky aroma and taste imparted during the smoking process elevates the flavor profile of brisket to new heights. Choosing the right wood adds layers of complexity to the meat. The creation of the beautifully caramelized bark adds further texture and an explosion of flavor with every bite. If you're new to smoking brisket, give yourself some grace. I have cooked thousands of briskets, and I am still learning.

Allow yourself to enjoy the process as much as the meat. Smoking brisket is an art that requires patience, skill, and attention to detail. The process involves selecting the right brisket, properly trimming it, wrapping it during cooking, mastering the holding phase, and ultimately slicing it to correct any errors that might have been made along the way. This recipe will walk you through each step of the journey, helping you achieve a mouthwatering, tender, and flavorful brisket that will leave you the envy of your family and friends.

SELECTING THE BRISKET

Choosing the right brisket is essential for a successful smoking session. Look for whole packaged brisket, which consists of two muscles—the flat and the point— separated by a layer of fat. When selecting the brisket, consider the following factors: (1) Size: The larger the brisket, the better it will cook. (2) Marbling: Select a brisket with good marbling, as this will ensure a juicier and more flavorful result. Wagyu is best, USDA prime is second best. (3) Thickness: Check for even thickness across the brisket, particularly the flat, as this promotes uniform cooking.

TRIMMING THE BRISKET

Properly trimming the brisket helps to achieve an even cooking process and prevents excessive fat rendering. Remove any excess fat from the fat side of the brisket, leaving about ¼-inch of fat to protect the meat. On the meat side of the brisket, trim off any thick fat patches and silver skin so the rub can adhere to the meat and create the bark. Trim any loose or hanging meat to ensure an even shape, promoting uniform cooking.

The goal is an aerodynamic brisket so when the heat travels over and around the brisket, it will not burn up any parts of the meat.

ADDITIONAL FLAVORS

Flavor enhancements to the brisket are a personal preference, so feel free to adjust different rubs, injections, woods, sauces, and quantities to suit your taste. Additionally, practice and experimentation are key to mastering the art of barbequing brisket.

Injection—Hydrolyzed protein is what you're looking for if using an injection. Hydrolyzed proteins are essentially proteins broken down into smaller, more easily absorbed peptides and amino acids. These smaller proteins are highly effective at binding water, which helps the meat hold on to moisture during the cooking process. This is crucial in barbeque, where long, slow cooking times can lead to meat drying out. Hydrolyzed proteins are stable under heat, meaning they won't break down as easily during cooking barbeque. In essence, hydrolyzed protein in meat injectors allows for better moisture retention, improved tenderness, and enhanced flavor, making it a key ingredient for achieving juicy, flavorful barbeque. If you'd like to use an injection, try Butcher BBQ or Kosmo.

Seasoning—I like using a base layer of kosher salt and fresh cracked black pepper. Then I like to go over the top with a light coating of G-Que Barbeque The Rub. After seasoning the brisket, I will let the brisket sit at room temperature for 30 minutes before placing in the smoker.

Saucing—The best time to sauce is after the rest. Sauce the uncut brisket and place back in the smoker for 25 minutes to let the sauce set. This will create a flavorful bark around the brisket.

Smoking Wood—Hickory is my favorite when smoking brisket, but oak and pecan woods work well too.

BEEF BRISKET

SERVES 15 TO 18

- 1 (15-pound) USDA prime brisket, trimmed
- ¼ cup kosher salt
- ¼ cup fresh cracked black pepper
- ½ cup G-Que Barbeque The Rub, or your favorite barbeque rub
- 2 ounces light beer

Prepare an outdoor smoker to 250°F with hickory.

Season the brisket on all sides with salt, pepper, and barbeque rub. Place the brisket in the smoker and cook until the brisket reaches an internal temperature of 160°F and the bark has been set and formed (times vary so keep an eye on the temperature and the meat). It's now time to wrap. Wrapping the brisket during the cooking process is a technique that helps retain moisture while enhancing tenderness. To help provide additional moisture, place the brisket inside butcher paper or heavy-duty aluminum foil and add the light beer. Be sure to wrap the brisket as tightly as possible to avoid extra air space inside the wrap.

The "stall" is a unique and sometimes perplexing phase that occurs when smoking a brisket (or other large cuts of meat, like pork shoulders). The stall refers to a temporary plateau in the internal temperature of the brisket during the cooking process. It's a crucial stage that can last for several hours, leading some to believe their meat is not progressing as it should. The stall typically occurs when the brisket's internal temperature reaches 150°F to 160°F. At this point, moisture starts evaporating from the surface of the meat. The moisture on the surface absorbs a significant amount of heat from the smoker, which temporarily slows down the rise in internal temperature of the brisket. This is precisely why we like to wrap and increase temperature and plow through the stall.

After wrapping the brisket and returning it to the smoker, increase the temperature 25 degrees to 275°F. This will help surge through the stall and prevent a dry brisket. I advise against increasing the temperature more than 25 degrees as you want to give yourself a large window to pull your brisket off without overcooking it.

The biggest mistake I see beginners make is they cook to a certain temperature or for a set period of time. The brisket will be done when it is done.

Once your brisket reaches an internal temperature of 200°F, begin to probe the flat of the brisket with your digital thermometer against the grain. When it feels like you're probing into Jell-O, the brisket is done. It's important to probe in the center of the flat against the grain every time as you will get different feels depending on whether or not you're with or against the grain; outside of the brisket versus the middle of the brisket or probing into a fat pocket will all give different results. Make sure you're comparing the same feel and not being misled by the variables I just mentioned above.

Once the brisket reaches the desired tenderness, it's time to hold (rest) the brisket before serving. This step is critical for keeping the meat juicy and preserving the flavor.

Begin by letting the brisket breathe. This also stops the cooking process. Open the foil and let the meat cool at room temperature for 15 minutes. Then wrap the cooked brisket with all its juices. Place the wrapped meat in a clean, insulated cooler or a preheated oven set to the lowest possible temperature, like 140°F. If your oven doesn't go that low, use an empty cooler. If using a cooler, add towels or blankets for extra insulation, especially if you're outside and it's cold. Hold the brisket for at least 3 to 4 hours. This resting period, during which time the meat drops from its cooked temperature of around 205°F down to 140°F, allows the juices to be reabsorbed and redistributed, resulting in a more succulent final product. If you can rest your brisket for 8 hours, even better, so long as it doesn't drop below 140°F. Once the meat hits 140°F, it's time to slice.

Properly slicing the brisket is the final step. Start by slicing the brisket across the grain of the meat on the flat end. This will result in tender, easy-to-chew slices. If you notice your brisket is over cooked, slice a little thicker and cut a little with the grain. If the brisket is slightly undercooked, slice thinner and go perpendicular against the grain. You can correct any errors made during the cook by adjusting your slices.

Arrange the slices on a serving platter, showcasing the beautiful smoke ring and bark. Use a fat separator to separate the fat from the foil juices and pour the juice over the sliced brisket. For additional flavor, add a little barbeque sauce to the brisket juice.

AND THERE YOU HAVE IT, THE PERFECT BRISKET READY TO ENJOY!

COMPETITION BRISKET & BURNT ENDS

SERVES 15 TO 18

Brisket Injection

2 cups water

1 tablespoon Minor's Beef Base

1 tablespoon Minor's Au Jus Base

½ cup Butcher Barbeque Prime Brisket Injection

1 (15-pound) Wagyu brisket, fat trimmed on meat-side only

½ cup fajita seasoning

G-Que Barbeque The Rub, or your favorite barbeque rub, as needed

Braise

2 tablespoons G-Que Original Barbeque Sauce, or your favorite barbeque sauce

1 (12-ounce) bottle Coors Light beer

½ cup apple cider vinegar

½ cup water

½ cup Worcestershire sauce

¼ cup olive oil

2 tablespoons G-Que Barbeque Hottish Sauce, or your favorite hot barbeque sauce

1 tablespoon Better than Bouillon Roasted Beef Base

Brisket is more than just a delicious meal. It represents the heart and soul of barbeque. Perfecting a brisket requires patience, precision, and a deep understanding of the meat and the smoking process. It's a labor of love that demands respect for tradition and a willingness to learn and adapt. Winning RMBBQA Team of the Year and top Brisket Cook was a culmination of years of hard work, late nights tending the smoker, and countless tweaks to my technique and recipes. It's a testament to the relentless dedication required to the craft of smoking brisket. Now when I prepare a competition brisket, it takes me back to the competitive barbeque circuit, where the camaraderie, the challenge, and the pursuit of perfection fueled my passion.

Begin by making the Brisket Injection: Add the water, beef base, and au jus base to a small saucepan over medium heat. Stir and heat until dissolved. Remove from heat and add the Butcher Barbeque Prime Brisket Injection. Stir until dissolved, then refrigerate the injection overnight. You should have about 2 cups of Injection.

Inject the Brisket Injection into the brisket using a syringe, starting on the flat and perpendicular to the grain of the meat. Inject every 2 inches or so. You will see the meat balloon up with each injection following a checkerboard pattern. Keep injecting until you've used up all the Injection, trying to spread it out evenly. The entire brisket should be ballooned up at this point.

Season the brisket with a light coat of fajita seasoning then season with a medium coat of the barbeque rub. Apply the rub on all sides of the brisket, pressing the rub into the meat to ensure it adheres well. Wrap the seasoned brisket in plastic wrap and refrigerate for 4 hours. One hour before cooking, remove the brisket from the refrigerator and plastic wrap and add a light coating of barbeque rub. Let the brisket rest at room temperature.

Prepare the smoker to 250°F with hickory wood.

Add the brisket to the smoker and smoke until the internal temperature of the brisket reaches 160°F (times vary so keep an eye on the temperature and the meat).

Remove the brisket and place, fat-side down, on two sheets of heavy-duty aluminum foil. Curl up the sides of the foil, which will help to make sure the braise doesn't spill out. Mix all ingredients for the Braise together. Pour the Braise into the foil until it reaches but does not cover the top of the brisket. Increase the smoker to 275°F. Wrap the brisket tightly and return to the smoker. Cook until the internal temperature of the brisket reaches 200°F. Remove the brisket, open the foil, and let vent for 15 minutes to stop the cooking process. Wrap the brisket again and let rest in a dry, empty cooler or insulated box for at least 1 hour. This allows the juices to reabsorb and results in a more tender brisket.

Burnt Ends

When the brisket is resting and you are about 1 hour away from wanting to serve the brisket, it's time to separate the point from the flat and create some fantastic burnt ends. To do so, cube the point into 1-inch cubes and season with the barbeque rub. Return the cubes to the smoker set at 275°F and cook for 30 to 35 minutes, or until the rub creates a light bark around the cubes. Remove the cubes and sauce the burnt ends with a 50/50 blend of the barbeque sauces. Return the sauced cubes to the smoker and cook for 20 minutes, or until the sauce is set up on the cubes. Remove from the smoker.

To serve, remove the brisket from the foil, reserving the liquid. Slice the flat of the brisket against the grain and arrange the slices on a serving platter. Mix 1 cup of the reserved liquid with 2 tablespoons of barbeque sauce and lightly brush or pour over the brisket slices. Add the Burnt Ends next to the slices and serve.

CHAMPIONS CORNER

This is not like the brisket you get at your favorite barbeque restaurant. This is competition brisket, meaning you need to impress the judges with one bite. The judges have already been sampling a lot of barbeque, and the time they get to brisket, it's the last of the four meats that gets judged. You need to wake up their taste buds and say, "Hello, here I am!"

BEEF BRISKET BURNT ENDS
(IN HALF THE TIME)

SERVES 6 TO 10 (DEPENDING ON THE SIZE OF THE BRISKET POINT)

1 (3- to 5-pound) USDA Prime beef brisket point muscle

½ cup G-Que Barbeque The Rub, or your favorite barbeque rub

1 cup G-Que Barbeque Hottish Sauce, or your favorite barbeque sauce, warmed

4 ounces beer, preferably Coors (or you can use beef broth)

Traditionally, and as seen in most barbeque competitions, the entire brisket, which includes the point and flat, gets smoked. When the meat is finished, the pitmaster will often cube up the point, season it, and put it back on the smoker for about 45 minutes to make burnt ends. This recipe offers a little trick to make burnt ends in half the time. We do so by first separating the point from the flat and then slicing the point into cubes, so each burnt end cooks individually, not as the entire point cut of meat. When making burnt ends at home, I prefer to use a drum smoker (page 21), as it cooks faster than any pellet or offset smoker. If you don't have a drum smoker, any smoker will work, so long as you can crank up the heat to 350°F as we're going to cook these relatively fast.

Prepare a drum smoker to 350°F using hickory wood.

If you have a whole brisket, separate the point from the flat. Once separated, trim the brisket point by removing any hard fat around the point. After all the fat has been removed, slice the point into 2-inch cubes. Lightly season the cubes with barbeque rub. Ensure all sides are covered, then place the seasoned cubes onto a wire rack, leaving a little space between each cube. Note: This step will allow the bark to form on all sides, offering a more flavorful bite. Place the rack with the cubes in the smoker and smoke until the internal temperature of the meat reaches 185°F, about 40 minutes.

Remove the burnt ends from the smoker and transfer them to a sheet of heavy-duty foil. Pour the beer over the top of the burnt ends and wrap the foil tightly. Wrap again with another sheet of foil (double wrap) to avoid any accidental

punctures. Return the wrapped burnt ends to the smoker and smoke until the internal temperature of the meat reaches 210°F, or until they're extremely tender, about 30 minutes. Remove the burnt ends, dunk them in warmed barbeque sauce, and place them back onto the wire rack and into the smoker for 25 minutes, or until the sauce is set. Remove the burnt ends from the smoker and let them rest for 5 minutes before serving.

CHAMPIONS CORNER

To remind, when purchasing beef, such as brisket, I recommend selecting USDA Prime. Beef gets graded by the USDA as either Select, Choice, or Prime. Prime is considered the best of the best. Usually, 7% of graded beef receives a prime rating, depending on the season and year. Personally, I find there's a huge difference between prime and choice in terms of flavor. That's because prime has more marbling (fat), which gives the meat that exceptional taste.

COMPETITION RIBS

SERVES 5 TO 6 (2 RIBS PER PERSON)

- 1 rack St. Louis pork spareribs
- ¼ cup canola oil
- G-Que Barbeque The Rub, or your favorite barbeque rub, as needed
- ½ cup packed dark brown sugar
- 2 tablespoons honey, divided
- ½ stick unsalted butter, divided
- ¼ teaspoon cayenne pepper
- 6 tablespoons apple juice
- ¼ cup G-Que Barbeque Hottish Sauce, or your favorite hot barbeque sauce
- ¼ cup G-Que Original Barbeque Sauce, or your favorite barbeque sauce
- 1 tablespoon peach preserves
- 1 teaspoon apple cider vinegar

St. Louis-style pork ribs are a specific cut of pork ribs that are trimmed from the spare ribs. They are known for their uniform shape, which makes them easier to cook evenly and present nicely. This is probably the cut of ribs that gets turned in at professional KCBS contests 85% of the time.

St. Louis-style ribs are cut from the full spare rib rack. The sternum, cartilage, and rib tips are removed to create a rectangular and uniform rack. This trim results in a neater and more consistent shape, making them a favorite among barbeque competitors seeking to impress with just one bite.

While I will tweak my competition recipes from time to time, this rib recipe is my go-to and one which I have won with the most. I believe at the highest levels of competition barbeque, it is more about cooking the meat just right then it is adding the ingredients. You must get the texture of the ribs just right to win. Over the years, I've enjoyed sharing these ribs not only with the judges, but with the spectators, especially those who never had a competition rib before. During competition, by the time the judges get to my ribs, they have already judged six entries of chicken, and they will likely have had five other ribs besides mine, so I need to over season to make the ribs stick out on the palate. Keep in mind, these are not ribs you sit down and eat an entire rack of, as they will be sweeter than any rib you have had. Just a couple ribs will do the trick.

Prepare the smoker to 275°F using hickory wood.

Remove the membrane from the back of the ribs. Use a sharp knife to separate the end of the membrane from the ribs, then use a paper towel to pull on the corner of the membrane you just separated and remove the rest of the membrane. Removing

the membrane will allow the ribs to be tender while absorbing more flavor into the meat.

Lightly coat the ribs on all sides with canola oil, then season with a light coat of barbeque rub. Make sure not to over season the ribs.

Let the seasoned ribs sit for 20 minutes at room temperature, then apply another light coat of barbeque rub and let sit for 15 minutes. Place the ribs, meat-side up, in the smoker and cook until the internal temperature of the ribs reaches 160°F and the ribs have a nice dark bark formed (times vary so keep an eye on the temperature and the meat). Remove the ribs.

Lay down 2 large sheets of heavy-duty aluminum foil—large enough to wrap the ribs—and set the ribs on top, meat-side up. Add half the brown sugar in a thin layer on top of the ribs followed by a light coating of the barbeque rub, 1 tablespoon of honey, half the butter, and the cayenne pepper. Turn the ribs over and cover the bone side with the remaining brown sugar, another light coating of rub, along with the remaining honey and butter. Add the apple juice and tightly wrap and return to the smoker meat-side down.

Let the ribs smoke for one hour and then check with a toothpick in between the bones. You want it to feel like if you put a toothpick into Jell-O. Remove the ribs from the smoker and vent the ribs for 2 minutes to stop the cooking process. Tightly wrap the ribs again and let sit in the foil at room temperature to reabsorb the juice. Let rest for 30 minutes while you make the rib sauce.

To make the rib sauce, add the two barbeque sauces with the peach preserves and apple cider vinegar to a small saucepan and add to the smoker to warm and absorb a little smoke. After 15 minutes, mix the sauce and place back on the smoker for another 15 minutes.

Remove the ribs from the foil, reserving the juice, and brush the ribs on all sides with the barbeque sauce. Return the ribs, meat-side up, to the smoker and apply a very light coat of barbeque rub to the top. Let cook for 20 minutes to allow the sauce and rub to setup into the meat.

Remove the ribs from the smoker and set aside.

Mix the reserve juice and the leftover rib sauce in a 50/50 ratio. Then dunk the sides of the ribs into this newly created glaze. Let the ribs sit for 2 minutes so the glaze can be absorbed and serve.

CHAMPIONS CORNER

Resting the ribs for 30 minutes is critical to get the perfect texture the judges are looking for. Same with seasoning the ribs with the barbeque rub on three separate occasions. Use this recipe as a guide and experiment with different seasonings at different stages as well as different ingredients in the foil pouch. This is what makes barbeque fun—the constant tweaking until you have created the perfect rib.

PORK SPARERIBS

SERVES 3 TO 4

1 rack St. Louis spareribs, membrane removed

G-Que Barbeque The Rub, or your favorite barbeque rub, as needed

½ cup packed dark brown sugar

2 tablespoons honey

½ stick unsalted butter, cut into pats

3 ounces apple juice

½ cup G-Que Barbeque Hottish Sauce, or your favorite barbeque sauce

CHAMPIONS CORNER

I like to always remove the membrane from the back of the ribs for better seasoning penetration and to ensure the ribs are tender. For a twist on the barbeque sauce, take about 4 ounces of sauce and combine it with 2 ounces of rib juice, and mix it together to make a delicious barbeque-au jus sauce to serve warm alongside the ribs.

If this is your first time smoking pork ribs, or you've been unsuccessful in the past, this tried-and-true recipe and method is a great place to start. The technique and combination of flavors shared below will help you achieve the proper rib color, tenderness, and taste that is sure to please.

Prepare an outdoor smoker to 275°F using hickory wood. Season both sides of the ribs as well as the inch on the top and the bottom with barbeque rub. Place the ribs in the smoker and smoke for 3½ hours, or until the bark is set (meaning, if you try to remove the rub with your finger it won't come off). The ribs should have nice mahogany color and be somewhat tender at this stage. Place the ribs on a sheet of heavy-duty aluminum foil. Add a light coat of barbeque rub on both sides of the ribs, along with a light coat of brown sugar to both sides. Drizzle both sides of the ribs with honey and add half the butter to each side along with the apple juice. Tightly wrap the ribs in the foil, making sure none of the liquids are seeping out. Note: It's very important to wrap the ribs as tightly as possible. Wrap again with another sheet of foil (double wrap) to avoid any accidental punctures. Return the ribs to the smoker. Check after 30 minutes for doneness. Open the foil package and use a toothpick to probe for tenderness. There should be very little resistance when you insert the toothpick into the meat of the rib. If you like your ribs super fall-off-the-bone (as opposed to having a little tug when eating the meat from the bone), wrap the ribs back up and return them to the smoker. Check every 20 minutes, or until the ribs are the way you like them. Once the ribs are ready, remove them from the smoker and open the foil package. Let the ribs sit for 5 minutes to vent the hot air. Brush both sides of the ribs with barbeque sauce and place them back in the smoker (no foil) for 15 minutes. Remove the ribs from the smoker, slice between each bone, and serve.

EASY PULLED PORK

SERVES 8 TO 10

- 1 (8-pound) Boston butt/pork butt, bone-in
- ¾ cup G-Que Barbeque The Rub, or your favorite barbeque rub
- ½ cup water
- ½ cup G-Que Original Barbeque Sauce, or your favorite barbeque sauce
- ¼ cup apple juice

Pulled pork is one of the most iconic dishes in barbeque, and it's typically made from a specific cut of pork that's perfect for slow cooking. The most common cuts of pork used for pulled pork are from the shoulder region of the pig, which has the right balance of fat and connective tissue to break down during slow cooking, resulting in tender, juicy meat.

Despite the confusing name, the Boston butt doesn't come from the rear of the pig. It comes from the upper part of the front shoulder. The term dates to colonial America. In New England, particularly in Boston, this cut of pork was packed in barrels known as "butts" for storage and shipping. The Boston butt is well-marbled with fat and contains a good amount of connective tissue, which makes it ideal for slow-cooking methods like smoking or braising. The intramuscular fat keeps the meat moist and flavorful during long cooks, making it perfect for pulled pork.

A typical Boston butt weighs between 5 to 10 pounds, though it can vary. It may or may not contain part of the blade bone. I always want a butt that has the bone. This cut becomes incredibly tender and easy to shred when cooked low and slow. The fat and connective tissue melt into the meat, giving pulled pork its rich, juicy texture and porky flavor.

The picnic shoulder (or picnic roast) comes from the lower part of the shoulder, below the Boston butt. This cut includes part of the shoulder joint and extends down toward the front leg.

The picnic shoulder is generally tougher than the Boston butt and has a bit more connective tissue. Picnic shoulders are typically larger than Boston butts, ranging from 6 to 12 pounds. It can come with the skin on, which adds flavor and crispiness if cooked with the skin intact.

You put them both together and you have the whole shoulder.

If you are new to smoking meat and would like to know the most forgiving meat to smoke, pulled pork is it. Follow this recipe and you will discover a foolproof delicious way to serve pulled pork at your next barbeque without having to trim or inject.

Preheat your drum smoker to 275°F with lump charcoal and hickory wood.

Season the pork butt with a medium coat of barbeque rub and then place in the smoker. We are going to let the pork cook until it reaches an internal temperature of 170°F and the bark is set up and has a nice mahogany color (times vary so keep an eye on the temperature and the meat). When the pork reaches the correct temperature and color, remove the pork from the smoker and place it on a sheet of heavy-duty aluminum foil. Add the apple juice (this also helps create some steam while the pork continues to cook). Wrap the pork tightly inside the aluminum foil then place it back onto the smoker until fork tender. Use a digital thermometer or temperature probe to check the pork when the meat reaches 200°F. When you're pleased with the texture of the pork and it's nice and tender, remove from the smoker, and open the foil to let the meat vent for about 10 minutes. This will help stop the cooking process.

After 10 minutes of venting, close the pork back up and wrap tightly to make sure no heat escapes. Let it rest for at least 30 minutes. Note: If time allows, let the pork keep resting for 1 to 2 hours. I recommend wrapping the foiled pork in a towel and then in a small cooler if you're going to let it go for more than 1 hour. Longer rests are one of the tricks to delicious championship barbeque.

While the pork is resting, add the water and barbeque sauce to a saucepot over very low heat to warm the ingredients. Be careful not to overheat or cook the sauce.

Remove the pork from the foil. The meat should be even more tender than it was when you pulled it off the smoker. Remove the bone and begin hand pulling all the fat away. Be mindful not to shred it. The ideal pull should be the size of both your thumbs together. We want the pork to have a nice mouth feel and two thumb chunks of pork will give you that. Once you have your pork pulled, add the warm water-barbeque sauce and mix it into the mix. Then give the pork a light dusting of barbeque rub and you are ready to serve.

CHAMPIONS CORNER

By adding that finishing sauce (water and barbeque sauce) at the end, you keep your pork moist while adding a touch more flavor. I find this technique works great at home when I'm having friends and family over. The pork stays moister longer, allowing my guests the ability to graze on the pork throughout the day.

JALAPEÑO-CHEDDAR SAUSAGE

SERVES 6

6 jalapeño cheddar sausages

If you've heard the phrase, "That's how sausage is made," you know it's a labor of love and a process that can be quite time consuming. To make sausage correctly, where it's juicy, tender, and snaps when you bite it like a crisp carrot, you're looking at a three-day process requiring a lot of time and machinery, including a meat grinder and sausage stuffer, which I'm sure many of you reading this may not have. Therefore, I'm not going to teach you how to make such sausage, but rather how to cook it once it's made. Visit your local butcher or gourmet markets, and you'll find a variety of delicious, homemade sausages. Innovation in sausage making has also led to the creation of many different flavors. My personal favorite is the jalapenño cheddar sausage. I find it has the right amount of heat and smoke, and the bits of cheddar add a nice creamy touch.

Smoking sausages brings out their full potential, with each component playing a role in delivering bold, satisfying flavors and textures. The fat in sausage is key, as it melts slowly during smoking, basting the meat from within and infusing it with rich, savory flavor. This fat also captures and carries the smoky notes from the wood, embedding them deep into the sausage for a flavor that's both intense and balanced. The casing, meanwhile, transforms in the heat, creating that beloved "snap" that gives a satisfying crunch with each bite. This crispy outer layer contrasts perfectly with the tender, juicy meat inside, where the slow-smoking process ensures the sausage is evenly cooked and full of moisture. A smoked sausage like jalapeño cheddar takes these elements even further, as the melting cheddar blends into the sausage, adding creamy pockets of flavor that pair beautifully with the kick of jalapeño. The result is a harmonious mix of smoky, spicy, and savory flavors, with textures that keep you coming back for more.

Prepare an outdoor smoker to 275°F.

Add the sausages and smoke until the internal temperature of the sausages reach 155°F.

CHAMPIONS CORNER

The key to juicy sausages is making sure not to overcook them. Use a meat thermometer to ensure the sausages reach the correct internal temperature.

SANDWICHES

Now that you've mastered the classic barbeque meats, it's time to serve some of your mouthwatering barbeque in sandwich form. I find this to be a satisfying way to showcase the smoky, savory flavors of classic barbeque meats. Beef brisket, pulled pork, sausage, and smoked turkey is what you'll discover in this chapter that make terrific and hearty sandwiches. The secret to a perfect barbeque sandwich lies not just in the meat but in the balance of flavors and textures.

Always begin with a sturdy, yet soft bun that can hold up to the juiciness of the meat. For our pulled pork sandwiches, slow-cooked pork shoulder is shredded and piled high on the bun, often topped with tangy coleslaw for a refreshing crunch. A drizzle of barbeque sauce adds a sweet or spicy kick, depending on your preference.

Brisket sandwiches are equally indulgent. Slices of smoky, tender brisket are layered on the bun, often with pickles, onions, and a rich sauce to complement the deep, beefy flavors. For an extra kick, some might add jalapeños or a creamy horseradish sauce.

Sausage sandwiches, too, are a flavorful option. Grilled or smoked sausage links are sliced and stuffed into rolls, paired with mustard, pickles, or onions for a savory bite. Whether serving to family or friends, these homemade barbeque sandwiches are sure to be a hit.

BEEF BRISKET ("THE MELTDOWN")

SERVES 1

- ½ pound cooked Beef Brisket (page 52)
- 1 toasted brioche bun
- ¼ cup G-Que Barbeque Hottish Sauce, or your favorite barbeque sauce, optional
- ½ cup Cheese Sauce (page 146)
- 2 large Bacon Onion Rings (page 132)

Inspired by the iconic Z-Man sandwich at Joe's Kansas City Barbeque The Original Gas Station Restaurant, this is how we make The Meltdown. If you are a fan of cheeseburgers, you will love The Meltdown. Beef brisket is slow-smoked until tender, then loaded with hot, melty cheese sauce and crispy beer-battered onion rings. This is my favorite item on the G-Que menu.

Stack the brisket on the bottom bun. No need to be stingy. If you like a big sandwich, pile on the brisket. Add the barbeque sauce, if using, pour the cheese sauce over the meat, add the onion rings, and crown the sandwich with the top bun.

CHAMPIONS CORNER

Different individuals like different toppings on their sandwich. Experiment and see what you and your guests like. I like to add sliced jalapeño cheddar sausage and some kettle chips, which I'll crumble for added texture and crunch.

BEEF BRISKET AND SAUSAGE
("THE SASQUATCH")

MAKES 1 SANDWICH

- ½ cup sliced cooked Beef Brisket (page 52)
- 1 toasted brioche bun
- 1 Jalapeño Cheddar Sausage (page 74)
- ¼ cup G-Que Barbeque Hottish Sauce, or your favorite barbeque sauce
- ½ cup Apple Slaw (page 90)

When it comes to barbeque sandwiches at G-Que, The Sasquatch turns heads with its sheer size. This sandwich marries the smoky tenderness of brisket with the spicy richness of jalapeño cheddar sausage, all topped with crisp, refreshing apple slaw. It's the perfect balance of flavors and textures, making every bite a delicious experience. This sandwich is not just a meal, it's a celebration of barbeque proficiency.

Assemble the sandwich by placing the brisket slices on the bottom bun. Slice the sausage in half lengthwise then slice the halves across the middle, giving you four pieces of sausage that should stack comfortably on top of the brisket. Add the barbeque sauce then the Apple Slaw and crown with the top bun and serve.

CHAMPIONS CORNER

Prepare the slaw just before assembling the sandwich to keep it fresh and crunchy. Also use quality brioche buns, which can hold up to the hearty fillings without getting soggy.

PULLED PORK ("THE CAROLINA")

MAKES 2 SANDWICHES

- 2 hamburger buns
- 10 ounces Easy Pulled Pork (page 70)
- 1 tablespoon of G-Que Barbeque Rub, or your favorite barbeque rub
- 1 cup Apple Slaw (page 90)
- ½ cup G-Que Barbeque Hottish Barbeque Sauce, or your favorite hot barbeque sauce, optional

The Carolina is our signature pulled pork sandwich we serve at G-Que Barbeque. We love this sandwich so much we offer it free for folks wanting to try it. The sandwich, with smoky pulled pork piled high and topped with a tart vinegar-based apple slaw, is the quintessential barbeque sandwich. The slaw perfectly complements the sweet barbeque sauce while the bits of tart Granny Smith apple provide texture and a nice contrast to the tender pork. I love this sandwich with our Hottish Barbeque Sauce for that extra zing.

Toast the hamburger buns by placing them on top of a preheated grill top or smoker for a couple minutes, or until the buns get light brown in color.

Starting with the toasted bottom bun, assemble the sandwich by adding half of the Pulled Pork to the bottom bun then season with half the rub. Add half of the G-Que Barbeque Hottish Sauce, if using, followed by half of the Apple Slaw. Top with the toasted bun and repeat to make the second sandwich.

CHAMPIONS CORNER

It's important to add the barbeque sauce to the meat and not on top of the slaw. Otherwise, you basically create a barbeque-laced slaw, and I don't find that as delicious.

16

SIGNATURE TURKEY SANDWICH
("THE PILGRIM")

MAKES 1 SANDWICH

- 2 cups frozen cranberries
- ½ cup granulated sugar
- ½ cup orange juice
- 1 tablespoon orange zest
- ¼ teaspoon ground cinnamon
- ¼ cup Garlic Mashed Potatoes (page 100)
- 1 toasted brioche bun
- 2/3 cup sliced Smoked Turkey Breast (page 230)

While The Meltdown is our most popular sandwich on the G-Que menu, The Pilgrim is my wife Heidi's favorite. This sliced turkey sandwich with cranberry relish and mashed potatoes is the ultimate comfort food, bringing together the best flavors of a classic holiday feast in a handheld delight. This recipe is perfect for using up holiday leftovers or simply enjoying a taste of Thanksgiving any time of year.

Add the cranberries, sugar, and orange juice to a saucepan over medium heat. Cook until the cranberries burst, and the mixture thickens, about 10 minutes. Stir in the zest and cinnamon and cook for 2 minutes allowing the flavors to come together. Remove from the heat and let cool before serving.

Assemble the sandwich by adding the Garlic Mashed Potatoes to the bottom brioche bun. Add slices of the Smoked Turkey, followed by the cranberry relish and crown with the top bun and serve.

CHAMPIONS CORNER

Use leftover turkey from a holiday meal or smoke a fresh turkey breast. Thinly sliced, juicy turkey is key to a delicious sandwich. Making your own cranberry relish adds a fresh, tangy contrast to the savory turkey and creamy mashed potatoes.

SIDES

Barbeque isn't just about the meat—great side dishes are essential to a complete experience. I've learned the right sides elevate the flavors coming off the smoker. A tangy slaw balances rich brisket; creamy mac and cheese adds comfort; pit smoked beans bring sweet, smoky depth. Each side complements and contrasts the main attraction, offering texture, variety, and personality to the plate. They tell a story about tradition, region, and taste. People remember the whole meal, not just the ribs. Done right, sides make your barbeque unforgettable and keep guests coming back for more every time.

GRILLED GARLIC BREAD WITH RICOTTA AND HONEY

SERVES 6

- 1 cup whole milk ricotta cheese
- 2 tablespoons fresh mint
- 4 tablespoons olive oil, divided
- 3 teaspoons honey
- Fresh ground sea salt, to taste
- Fresh cracked black pepper, to taste
- 1 loaf rustic Italian bread, sliced
- 2 cloves garlic, peeled

Obtain the freshest ricotta you can find. Do not skimp on the fat content either. The fresher and creamier the ricotta is, the better it's going to whip into a light and creamy dip. Choose a high-quality, rustic Italian or sourdough loaf for the best texture and flavor. Experiment with different types of honey. Clover honey is a mild option, while wildflower or acacia honey can add unique floral notes. For added texture, sprinkle some toasted nuts, like pine nuts or chopped almonds, over the ricotta spread.

I enjoy serving this delicious bread as a starter or side item. The rustic charm of grilled bread, the luxurious creaminess of ricotta, and the natural sweetness of honey make this dish come together so well. The dish also represents the joy of simple, high-quality ingredients brought together in harmony. The crisp, smoky edges of the grilled bread, infused with the rich aroma of garlic, provide a perfect contrast to the creamy, smooth texture of the ricotta. I hope you enjoy this recipe as it is one of my favorites.

Add the ricotta to a small mixing bowl. Using a hand mixer with whisk attachment, whisk the ricotta for 2 minutes, or until smooth and creamy. Place the whipped ricotta in a serving bowl and set aside.

Add the mint, 1 tablespoon olive oil, honey, and salt to a separate mixing bowl. Mix well until incorporated, then add the mixture on top of the whipped ricotta. Season with the pepper and set aside.

Prepare the grill for two-zone cooking (page 30). Brush the remaining 3 tablespoons olive oil on one side of the bread slices then place the slices over medium-high heat for 1 to 2 minutes on each side, or until toasted. Remove the slices from the heat and rub the garlic cloves around the edges and on top of the bread slices to infuse the garlic flavor while the bread is still hot.

Serve the bread slices with the bowl of ricotta-honey for dunking. You can also smear the spread onto the bread, whatever you and your guests prefer.

APPLE SLAW

MAKES 16 SERVINGS

- 1 large Granny Smith apple, cut into cubes (or matchsticks)
- 1 head of green cabbage, thinly sliced
- 5 cups thinly sliced red cabbage
- 1 medium carrot, julienned

Dressing

Makes 1 cup

- 1/2 cup granulated sugar
- 1 cup apple cider vinegar
- 1 teaspoon salt
- 1 teaspoon fresh cracked black pepper

Granny Smith has always been my go-to apple because of its tartness, but you can use a sweet apple if you'd like more sweetness in your slaw. For an extra touch of flavor, consider adding a handful of toasted walnuts or pecans. I'd only add the nuts if I was serving the slaw as a side.

Here's a refreshing, vibrant, and versatile slaw that offers a delightful blend of sweet and tangy flavors. I love it on its own as a mayo-free side or piled high atop a mountain of smoked pork for added crunch and taste. This is the recipe we've used at G-Que Barbeque for our Pulled Pork Sandwiches (page 82). The slaw complements the smoky notes of pulled pork and other grilled favorites and is a staple at my picnics and barbeques.

Combine the apples, cabbages, and carrots in a large mixing bowl. Set aside.

In a separate bowl, whisk together the sugar and vinegar until the sugar is completely dissolved. Season with the salt and pepper.

Pour the vinegar dressing over the slaw mixture. Toss gently but thoroughly to ensure all the ingredients are evenly coated with the dressing.

Cover the bowl with plastic wrap and refrigerate for at least 1 hour before serving. This will allow the flavors to meld and the vegetables to slightly soften, enhancing the overall texture and taste. Give the slaw a quick toss before serving to redistribute any dressing that has settled at the bottom.

HOMEMADE KETTLE CHIPS

SERVES 2

2 russet potatoes, peeling is optional, sliced ¼-inch thick

2 tablespoons olive oil

2 tablespoons G-Que Barbeque The Rub

Make sure your potato slices are of even thickness to ensure they cook at the same rate. Using a mandoline slicer can help achieve consistent slices. Potatoes can absorb a lot of oil, so don't skimp on the oil. The oil also helps to crisp the potatoes and carry the flavors of the seasonings. Potatoes can go from perfectly crispy to burnt in a matter of seconds. Keep an eye on them and adjust the placement as necessary to avoid charring. Feel free to change up the seasonings. Smoked paprika can add a different dimension of flavor, or try adding a dash of cayenne pepper for some heat. You can also elevate the potatoes by topping them with fresh shredded Parmesan cheese and herbs.

There's something irresistible about the simplicity and flavor of grilled potato chips. This recipe brings out the natural starch of the potatoes while adding a smoky, crispy exterior that's hard to beat. Perfect as a side dish for any barbeque feast, these homemade kettle chips are a crowd-pleaser that pairs well with anything, from steaks to burgers. The secret to their deliciousness lies in the balance of seasoning and the perfect grill technique, resulting in a potato side dish that's simple and full of flavor.

Prepare the grill for two-zone cooking (page 30).

Add the sliced potatoes and the oil to a mixing bowl. Toss until evenly coated then season the potatoes with barbeque rub. Toss again.

Arrange the potato slices directly on the grill and close the lid. Cook the potatoes until they are golden brown on one side, 6 to 10 minutes. Make sure the potatoes don't burn and adjust their placement on the grill as necessary.

Turn the potatoes over and cook until tender when pierced with a fork, and slightly crisp and golden brown on the outside. For extra crispy potatoes, let the potatoes cook on the direct (hot side) of the grill while flipping to ensure they don't burn.

Remove the potatoes from the grill, apply another coat of barbeque rub, or salt and pepper to taste, and serve.

PICKLED RED ONIONS

MAKES 1 CUP

1 cup peeled and thinly sliced red onion (about 1 medium onion)

1 cup white vinegar

3 tablespoons granulated sugar

1½ tablespoons salt

2 tablespoons black peppercorns

1 garlic clove, peeled and smashed

The beauty of this recipe lies in its simplicity and the room for customization. It's also a testament to how simple ingredients can come together to create a wonderful condiment that elevates the dish it accompanies. Feel free to adjust the sugar level depending on your preference for sweetness or add more vinegar for that extra tang. Apple cider vinegar works well too. If you like garlic add more garlic, or some red pepper flakes if you prefer a little heat.

Have you ever sliced onions to use for burgers or sandwiches and wound up with leftover onion? This quick recipe, which we make regularly at G-Que Barbeque, will make excellent use of the extra. For those of you who visit barbeque restaurants across the country, you're probably familiar with pickled red onions. They're vibrant, tangy, and enhance other dishes with a unique taste and texture. Sliced thinly and submerged in an easy-to-make brine, the onions undergo a transformation, turning from sharp and pungent—sometimes overpowering—to mellow and sweet with the perfect amount of tang and crunch. This versatile condiment is terrific on hamburgers, hot dogs, tacos, cold-cut sandwiches, or mince them to top a mile high plate of nachos. Anytime you're looking to add some color and zing to a dish, reach for these pickled red onions.

Add the vinegar, sugar, salt, and peppercorns to a saucepot over medium-high heat. Bring to a boil while whisking to dissolve the sugar and salt.

Now you have a decision to make: If you like your onions soft, add them to the boiling mixture for 2 to 3 minutes to soften. Then turn off the heat and let the mixture cool before pouring everything into a Mason jar (or other non-reactive container) and add the garlic. If you like your onions with texture and crunch, do not cook the onions. Instead, place the sliced onions and garlic directly in a Mason jar and pour the cool liquid over the top. Make sure the pickling liquid covers all the onions. Tightly seal the lid and give it a good shake. This will distribute the vinegar mixture and flavorings evenly among the onions. Let the onions pickle for at least one day before using as the flavors will continue to develop over time. The pickled onions, if sealed in the jar and reserved in the refrigerator, will last up to six months, although it's best if enjoyed within one month.

PIT-SMOKED BEANS

SERVES 10 TO 12

- 2 (15-ounce) cans pinto beans
- 1 (15-ounce) can black beans
- 1 cup (or more) G-Que Original Barbeque Sauce, or your favorite sauce
- 4 ounces G-Que Barbeque The Rub, or your favorite barbeque rub
- Light beer, as needed, for moisture when cooking
- ½ pound brisket, sausage, or pulled pork (or whatever meat you prefer)

Pit-Smoked Beans are a quintessential side dish in barbeque, offering depth, richness, and the soul-satisfying taste and comforting aroma that only comes from low and slow cooking. This easy recipe captures the essence of true barbeque: patience, technique, and the pursuit of flavor that lifts simple ingredients into something extraordinary. At G-Que Barbeque, we cook our beans on the smoker under our baby back ribs. The magic unfolds as the beans catch and absorb the pork drippings while developing a robust, smoky goodness from the hickory wood. Keep in mind when making this hearty dish at home, if you use a thick barbeque sauce, your beans will have a thick consistency; a thinner sauce, the thinner the bean mixture. The trick is getting just the right amount of gooeyness, which will come with practice after you've made this recipe a few times.

Open the cans of beans, strain the juice, and rinse the beans under cold water. Add them to an aluminum foil pan (12½" ×10¼" × 2½") and add enough barbeque sauce to coat the beans. Stir well to incorporate the sauce with the beans. Then add a thin, even layer of rub on top of the beans.

Place the pan of beans in a preheated smoker set between 225°F and 275°F (or on the indirect side of a barbeque or gas grill, the idea being that you'll be cooking in conjunction with your direct cook). Close the lid and let the beans cook slowly for about 4 hours. Check periodically and stir gently each time. If the mixture is getting too thick or absorbing the liquid too quickly, add a bit of light beer to keep the beans moist and prevent burning. If you can cook the beans under your meats, which is how we do it, go ahead and do so like I mentioned in the headnote; the drippings from the meat will add terrific moisture and flavor to the beans.

The beans are done when they are tender, and the sauce has thickened to your liking. Then add some of the cooked meat to the beans and stir to incorporate. Adjust the seasoning by adding more rub if necessary. Serve hot.

CHAMPIONS CORNER

For a splash of heat to your beans, add a little hot sauce. I prefer Tapatio. When it comes to adding the meat to the beans, I prefer chunks of brisket from the flat while leaving the point to be enjoyed on its own. I've also added Jalapeño Cheddar Sausage (page 74) and it's fantastic.

HISTORY OF PIT-SMOKED BEANS

Pit-Smoked Beans, commonly referred to as barbeque beans, are a staple of American cuisine and have a rich history intertwined with the evolution of barbeque itself. The origins of barbeque beans trace back to Native American cooking methods, where beans were cooked slowly over open flames with ingredients like maple syrup or bear fat for flavor. Early European settlers adopted this cooking style and adapted it to include ingredients like molasses, pork fat, and salted meats.

During the 19th century, barbeque became increasingly popular in the southern United States, particularly in regions like Texas, Kansas City, and the Carolinas. As barbeque culture flourished, so did the variety of side dishes served alongside smoked meats. Beans, inexpensive and readily available, became a natural complement to barbequed meats due to their hearty texture and ability to absorb flavors.

The popularity of barbeque beans continued to grow throughout the 20th century, becoming a fixture at backyard cookouts, family gatherings, and barbeque joints across the country. Recipes for barbeque beans evolved, incorporating regional variations such as the addition of mustard, vinegar, brown sugar, or even bourbon.

Today, barbeque beans remain a beloved dish in American barbeque culture, cherished for their smoky flavor, hearty texture, and ability to bring together the flavors of a traditional barbeque meal.

GARLIC MASHED POTATOES

SERVES 5 TO 6

- 1½ pounds red potatoes, skin on, halved
- 3 tablespoons unsalted butter
- ¾ cup sour cream
- ¼ cup whole milk
- ½ tablespoon minced garlic
- 1 teaspoon garlic powder
- Sea salt and fresh cracked black pepper, as needed, to taste

If you're looking for an easy-to-make potato recipe to satisfy your "meat and potato" craving, look no further. The addition of garlic gives these potatoes bold flavor while sour cream ensures smooth and creamy mashed potatoes. This delicious side is very similar to what we serve in the restaurant, but without the sour cream.

Add the potatoes to a large pot with enough water to cover the potatoes by 2 inches. Place the pot over high heat and bring to a boil. Once boiling, reduce the heat to medium-high. Cook until the potatoes are soft and to your liking, 8 to12 minutes. Drain and transfer the potatoes to a large bowl. Add the butter, sour cream, milk, garlic, garlic powder, and season with salt and pepper. Using a potato masher, mash the potatoes and ingredients until just combined. Note: Don't over-mash—you'll want some texture. Check and adjust the seasoning, if necessary, and serve.

CHAMPIONS CORNER

Feel free to customize your mashed potatoes by adding roasted garlic, cream cheese, heavy cream instead of milk, or even a bit of grated Parmesan cheese for extra flavor. Mashed potatoes can be made ahead of time and reheated in the oven. To reheat, place in an oven-safe dish, cover with foil, and heat at 350°F until warmed through, 20 to 30 minutes.

MAC 'N' CHEESE

SERVES 5

½ pound uncooked elbow macaroni

3 tablespoons salted butter

2 tablespoons all-purpose flour

½ teaspoon salt

½ teaspoon white pepper

1½ cups whole milk

¾ cup half and half

½ teaspoon G-Que Barbeque The Rub, or your favorite barbeque rub

2½ cups freshly shredded cheddar cheese, divided

Your choice of cheddar makes a difference. The higher the quality of cheese the better it will taste of course. Experiment with your favorite cheeses. I like cheddar and gruyère and will avoid mild cheeses as they have less flavor. Make sure to freshly grate the cheese. Pre-shredded store-bought cheese will not melt the same as freshly grated cheese. Also make sure to bring the cheese to room temperature before adding to the sauce. For the cheese to melt properly and smoothly, you want gradual changes in temperature.

Macaroni and cheese used to be a staple at barbeque restaurants, but these days I don't see it on menus as often. At G-Que Barbeque, our mac and cheese is still the best-selling side. We add a sprinkle of our barbecue rub and freshly grated cheddar to the mix for a flavor that keeps guests coming back. At home, I like to switch things up with Gruyère—a richer, more decadent cheese that takes the dish to another level.

Preheat the oven to 350°F.

Lightly grease an 8-inch (or similar size) baking dish and set aside.

Prepare the macaroni by bringing 4 to 6 quarts of water to a boil. Add salt to taste. Add the macaroni and stir gently. Return to a boil and cook, uncovered, stirring occasionally, for 8 minutes, or until al dente. Drain and set aside.

Make the cheese sauce by adding the butter to a medium saucepan over medium heat. When the butter has melted, stir in the flour, salt, and pepper. Cook for 2 minutes. Slowly add the milk and half and half, stirring constantly, and cook over medium-low heat until the mixture has thickened like the consistency of gravy, 5 to 7 minutes. Remove from the heat, let cool for several minutes, then stir in 1 cup shredded cheese, stirring just until melted; don't over stir. Add the cooked macaroni, barbeque rub, and toss to coat. Pour half of the pasta mixture into the prepared baking dish. Sprinkle ½ cup cheese over the top. Add the remaining pasta and cheese. Cook for 15 minutes, or until the cheese on top has melted.

CLASSIC RUBS & SAUCES

From my experience, I know a good rub builds the foundation—seasoning the meat, creating that perfect bark. It's where flavor begins. Sauces, on the other hand, bring it home—adding sweetness, heat, tang, or smoke depending on the style. They highlight and enhance, not overpower. Together, rubs and sauces define your barbeque's identity and make each bite something you remember long after the meal.

BARBEQUE RUB

MAKES ABOUT ½ CUP

¼ cup packed dark brown sugar

2 teaspoons kosher salt

2 teaspoons fresh cracked black pepper

2 teaspoons smoked paprika

1 teaspoon garlic powder

1 teaspoon onion powder

1 teaspoon ground mustard

½ teaspoon chipotle powder

½ teaspoon ancho chili powder

¼ teaspoon cayenne pepper

Over the years, I've experimented with countless rub variations, learning from each cookout and competition. For me, this traditional barbeque rub is more than a blend of spices—it's a reflection of my journey in the barbeque world. I encourage you to use this rub recipe as a base and revise the ingredients to make it your own. Barbeque is as much about personal expression as it is about tradition. Feel free to tweak the ingredients to suit your taste preferences. Maybe you prefer a bit more heat or a touch of sweetness—go ahead and adjust the proportions. By experimenting and making it your own, you'll not only create a rub that you love, but you will embark on your own barbeque journey, discovering the unique flavors that will make your barbeque stand out.

Add all ingredients to a mixing bowl. Mix until incorporated and the brown sugar is finely broken up. Use immediately or store in an airtight container in a cool, dark place up to 6 weeks.

CHAMPIONS CORNER

If you'd like to make a versatile rub, use your favorite barbeque rub and blend it with some seasoning salt. This is terrific on poultry and vegetables. If you'd like to tweak a rub toward beef, add more garlic, salt, and pepper and remove the sweet notes. Have fun and experiment with your barbeque rub. In general, a good all-purpose rub should be well balanced with sweet, heat, and a touch of savory. There shouldn't be any ingredients that stick out to where you can identify any overwhelming flavors.

BARBEQUE SAUCE

MAKES ABOUT 2 CUPS

- 2/3 cup ketchup
- 5 tablespoons apple cider vinegar
- ¼ cup packed dark brown sugar
- 1 tablespoon molasses
- 2 teaspoons smoked paprika
- 1 teaspoon ground cumin
- 1 teaspoon chili powder
- 1 teaspoon kosher salt
- 1 teaspoon fresh cracked black pepper
- ½ teaspoon cayenne pepper

Use high-quality ingredients, especially ketchup and vinegar. The base ingredients set the tone for the entire sauce. Adjust the thickness of the sauce by simmering it longer or adding a bit of water if it becomes too thick. The sauce should be thick enough to cling to the meat but not so thick that the sauce overpowers it. Let the sauce rest for at least 24 hours before using. This allows the flavors to meld and develop, resulting in a richer, more complex sauce.

Barbeque sauce is more than just a condiment—it's an integral part of the barbeque experience. I find creating a championship-winning barbeque sauce requires experimentation and an understanding of how ingredients affect the overall flavor of the sauce and how the flavor of the sauce will affect the taste of the meat when enjoyed. My strategy is to focus on the balance between sweetness, tanginess, and heat. I encourage you to use this recipe as a base and make gradual adjustments. This sauce works well with various meats, from ribs and brisket to chicken and pulled pork. Don't hesitate to experiment with it on different dishes to discover your personal favorite combinations.

In a medium saucepan, combine the wet ingredients, including the sugar. Stir to blend well and let cook for 5 minutes. Then add the seasonings. Stir to incorporate the dry ingredients into the sauce. Cook over medium heat and bring the mixture to a gentle simmer. Once it starts simmering, reduce the heat to low to prevent burning. Let the sauce simmer on low for 15 to 20 minutes, stirring occasionally. The sauce will thicken slightly as it cooks. If you prefer a thinner sauce, you can add water (a tablespoon at a time) until you reach your desired consistency. Taste the sauce after about 15 minutes and adjust the seasoning if needed. Add more brown sugar for sweetness, more vinegar for tang, or cayenne pepper for extra heat. Once the sauce has thickened and the flavors have melded, remove it from the heat. Let the sauce cool slightly before serving.

HONEY-LIME SRIRACHA SAUCE

MAKES 3¼ CUPS

½ cup melted butter

½ cup sriracha

2/3 cup Frank's RedHot sauce

¼ cup fresh lime juice

¼ cup white vinegar

1¼ cups honey

If you're a fan of sriracha, you must try this sauce on your next poultry dish. It's colorful and zesty and really pops with notes of sweet and citrus. At G-Que, we often use our Honey Lime Sriracha Sauce on our chicken wings as a "Wing Special" at the restaurant. I find the addition of Frank's RedHot really reinforces the red-orange color while offering a recognizable heat to balance the hand-crafted sauce.

Add all ingredients to a saucepan. Mix until combined and cook over indirect (medium) heat on your grill for 12 to 15 minutes, or until homogenized and warm. Note: Make sure not to cook over the hottest part of the grill or you'll scorch the sauce. Keep warm until ready to use.

CHAMPIONS CORNER

Since everyone has a different palate, adjust the taste to your liking. If you find the sauce too sweet, add a little more Frank's RedHot or sriracha. If the sauce isn't sweet enough, add a little more honey. Use this recipe, and pretty much all the recipes in this book, as a guideline and adjust to what you feel is perfect for you and your guests.

食品公司
FOODS, INC.

ELEV
SPEC

ATED
IALS

RECIPES

CRAFT COCKTAILS

Sipping cocktails at backyard barbeques or while smoking meats is all about complementing the smoky, savory flavors of such dishes with bold, refreshing drinks. Classic choices include bourbon-based cocktails, like my Bourbon Grilled Lemonade or Gentleman Jack and Pepsi, which pair well with the deep, rich flavors of smoked meats. For a lighter option, try my fruity Hangover Cure, which provides a bright, sweet contrast to the heaviness of barbeque sauces and rubs. Pick-me-up cocktails, like the classic Red Bull Vodka Spritz, are also popular. Ultimately, barbeque cocktails should enhance the casual, smoky atmosphere, making them refreshing yet strong enough to stand up to the bold flavors. Here are my favorites to get you going.

BOURBON-GRILLED LEMONADE

SERVES 6 TO 8

Honey Simple Syrup

½ cup granulated sugar

½ cup water

½ cup honey

6 pounds fresh lemons (about 24 regular-size lemons)

6 cups water

Bourbon, as needed

Fresh mint sprigs, for garnish

CHAMPIONS CORNER

Grilling lemons not only imparts a grilled flavor but also caramelizes the sugars, adding depth to the lemonade. For a non-alcoholic version, simply omit the bourbon.

Bourbon Grilled Lemonade offers a refreshing and sophisticated barbeque twist on America's summer classic, perfect for any barbeque or outdoor gathering. The bourbon's smooth warmth intertwines with the natural tartness and caramelized flavors of the grilled lemonade, offering a memorable cocktail that is both invigorating and satisfying. This spirited beverage is also one you'll likely encounter at a bonafide grill master's backyard.

Preheat an outdoor grill to medium-high heat.

Begin by making the Honey Simple Syrup: Add the sugar, water, and honey to a foil pan and place in one corner of the preheated grill. Allow to heat so the ingredients can dissolve into each other.

Meanwhile, cut the lemons in half and place, flesh-side down, on the grill. Grill until the flesh is golden-brown and caramelized. Note: If you're getting black grill marks on the lemons your grates are either not clean or too hot.

Remove the grilled lemons and the foil pan with the hot simple syrup. Using a juice squeezer, squeeze the juice from the lemon halves into a pitcher or suitable container. Note: Save some of the squeezed lemon halves for garnish. Add the water and Honey Simple Syrup. Stir well to combine and refrigerate until ready to serve.

To serve, fill a wide mouth, 32-ounce Mason jar with ice. That's right. Go big or go home. Add the chilled lemonade to the halfway mark. Top with the bourbon (or add as much bourbon as you like and fill the rest of the jar with more lemonade). Stir and garnish with a fresh mint sprig and one of the squeezed lemon halves.

FIRST POUR

MAKES 1 COCKTAIL

½ cup Gentleman Jack
½ cup Pepsi

Gentleman Jack is unique—do you know it's the only whiskey in the world mellowed twice through charcoal, once before and once after aging? This extra step gives it an exceptionally smooth finish. Crafted by Jack Daniel's, Gentleman Jack is a refined Tennessee whiskey that I find is perfect for sipping neat or in simple cocktails like this one.

During the early days of barbeque competition, I would arrive with my smoker, get my equipment into position, and begin setting up. After trimming all my meats and getting them inspected, I would make a First Pour and head over to the cooks' meeting where the judges went over the various rules and regulations. Making this drink was more than just a routine—it was a moment of reflection and anticipation. The familiar clunk of ice in the red Solo cup, popping the top off the whisky bottle, and the effervescent fizz of cola created a sensory experience that grounded me in the present and connected me to past barbeque competitions.

Today, the First Pour isn't just a drink—it is a companion, and a testament to the fun and passion that defined my barbeque journey. The drink also symbolizes the camaraderie and spirit of the barbeque community. Sharing a toast with fellow competitors, discussing strategies, and trading tips and secrets becomes part of the experience. The First Pour will always be more than just a nostalgic indulgence—it represents the joy of cooking, the thrill of competing, and the community that makes it all worthwhile.

Fill a red Solo cup with ice. Add the Gentleman Jack and Pepsi. Stir well, take a sip, and head on over to the cooks' meeting.

SPIRITED VODKA SPRITZ

MAKES 1 COCKTAIL

2 ounces vodka

4 ounces Red Bull

2 ounces Prosecco, or as needed

Lime wedge, for garnish

This timeless classic is still one of my all-time sippers. Between the smooth, crisp taste of vodka and the subtly sweet and invigorating kick of Red Bull, this drink delivers the energy boost I need during competitions to get all the way through to turn-ins. Sometimes at a competition I need a little pick-me-up from eating so much barbeque, and this cocktail does the trick. Enjoy one the next time you're craving a refreshing and energizing beverage. With this recipe, I take it a step further and add a splash of Prosecco for a little more effervescence.

Fill a pint glass with ice. Add the vodka and Red Bull. Top with Prosecco and stir to combine. Garnish with a lime wedge and serve.

CHAMPIONS CORNER

Use a high-quality vodka for a smoother taste. I also like to chill the Red Bull beforehand to keep the drink cold without diluting it with too much ice. For a sweeter sip, rim the glass with sugar.

G-QUE
BARBEQUE

HANGOVER CURE

SERVES 4

4 cups pineapple juice

1 cup orange juice

1 cup cream of coconut

4 ripe pineapples (1 for each person)

Strawberry rum, as needed, optional

Freshly grated nutmeg, as needed

Have you ever woken up after a heavy night of drinking and wished there was something to make you feel better? This recipe will take your pain away. I was introduced to this hangover cure when I was competing against a barbeque team from Denver, dubbed Pig Floyd. With only a few hours of sleep and lots of booze, I remember one Saturday morning, around the time the sun was coming up, the Pig Floyd crew swung by my tent and handed me a "painkiller cocktail" to nurse my wounds from the previous night. To this day, the refreshing drink continues to hit the spot. It's loaded with sweet, tropical fruit juices (Pig Floyd insists it's not the drink unless you use Simply Orange along with strawberry-infused rum). Thanks for all the painkillers, Pig Floyd. You guys rock!

Begin by making the mixer. Add the pineapple juice, orange juice, and cream of coconut to a one-gallon container. Seal and shake well. Set aside.

Core out each pineapple, removing all but about ½- inch around on the inside wall. Note: The more you carve out, the larger the "cup."

Fill each pineapple with ice. Fill halfway with the strawberry rum and then top with the reserved fruit juice mixture. Garnish with fresh grated nutmeg and serve with a straw. Note: For a non-alcoholic version, simply omit the rum.

UPSCALE STARTERS & ONE BITES

Barebeque starters are more than just a way to start the meal—they're the first impression, a small bite packed with flavor that sets the stage for everything that follows. For me, they're a celebration of what barbeque is all about: bold, smoky flavors, creativity, and bringing people together. They serve as a teaser for the main event, but they're also an opportunity to showcase a range of techniques and ingredients, each with the potential to surprise and delight your guests. Some of them I like so much I use as sides.

These recipes allow you to explore the versatility of barbeque. They offer a chance to play with flavors and textures that can be both familiar and inventive. These dishes invite your guests to take a moment to savor what's to come. I love the way appetizers set the mood—people gather around the grill or smoker, mingling, laughing, and sharing bites that spark conversation.

In this chapter, you'll find recipes designed to make your barbeque appetizers the talk of the party. From finger foods that are perfect for casual backyard gatherings to more refined bites that add elegance to any occasion, each recipe captures the heart of barbeque in its own way. You'll learn how to balance sweet, savory, and spicy flavors, and master techniques to get the most out of each ingredient. Expect to find everything from barbeque classics like pimento cheese and pork belly to more adventurous appetizers like pretzels and onion rings or beer chili in a bowl made from bacon, each one bursting with flavor and crafted to impress.

BACON-WRAPPED PRETZELS WITH CRAFT BEER CHEESE DIP

SERVES 4 TO 6

24 strips thin-cut bacon

G-Que Barbeque The Rub, or your favorite barbeque pork rub

12 pretzel rods

Craft Beer Cheese Dip

1 (12-ounce) bottle light and refreshing (not dark and heavy) craft beer

1 cup (8 ounces) cream cheese

1 pound shredded pepper jack cheese

G-Que Barbeque The Rub, or your favorite barbeque pork rub, optional

Choose a craft beer that complements the flavors of the bacon and cheese while trying to avoid thicker, darker beers like porters. For an extra touch, especially if you have your barbeque going, finish the Bacon Wrapped Pretzels on the grill for 2 or 3 minutes on each side to add a subtle smoky char.

When I first moved to Colorado, I would make this snack when my friends came over to watch our Colorado Buffalos and Denver Broncos. I also discovered it's a delicious bite most people haven't tried. Today, this easy recipe remains one of my go-tos for game days and tailgates. Imagine a combination of savory and salty flavors, heightened by the smoky essence of bacon. The crispy texture of the bacon further complements the doughy interior of the pretzel, creating a satisfying contrast. The addition of the Craft Beer Cheese Dip adds richness and depth, with the tanginess of the cheese blending seamlessly with the light, refreshing undertones of the beer. When making this at home, you'll want to use pretzel rods. They're thick and crunchy pretzels about 7- to 8-inches long. They come prepacked and you can find them at your local supermarket and online.

Preheat the oven or outdoor smoker to 325°F.

Begin by dusting both sides of the bacon with barbeque rub. Then wrap the seasoned bacon evenly around each pretzel rod, stopping about 1 inch from the end so your fingers have a place to hold the rod. Place the rods on a rack and transfer to the preheated oven or smoker. Cook the bacon, checking after 12 minutes, until the bacon is crispy. Remove the rods from the oven or smoker and let rest for 7 minutes to firm up. While the rods are resting, make the Craft Beer Cheese Dip.

Add the beer to a pot over medium heat and bring to a simmer. Add the cream cheese and cheese. Whisk, while cooking, until a cheese-sauce consistency is achieved. For a little extra zip, season with some extra barbeque rub, if desired. Remove the pot from the heat and transfer the sauce to a large cup. To serve, arrange the Bacon Wrapped Pretzels on a platter and serve with the warm Craft Beer Cheese Dip.

PIMENTO BACON CHEESE DIP

SERVES 8

- 2 pounds extra sharp cheddar cheese, freshly grated
- 1 cup Monterey Jack cheese, freshly grated
- 1 (4-ounce) jar pimentos, drained and diced
- ½ cup mayonnaise, plus more if needed
- 6 slices bacon, cooked and crumbled
- Salt and fresh cracked black pepper, to taste
- 1 tablespoon G-Que Barbeque The Rub, or your favorite Barbeque Rub

Savor this Southern staple with a G-Que Barbeque twist–crisp and crumbled bacon is mixed into a delicious pimento cheese dip, marrying tradition with decadence. Every spoonful is a luxurious meld of textures and flavors, designed to delight the senses. This isn't just pimento cheese, it's a celebration of opulence in every bite, an easy yet extravagant way to indulge in the finer flavors of life.

Add the cheeses, pimentos, mayonnaise, bacon, salt, pepper, and your rub to a large bowl. Mix until incorporated. Note: Add some additional mayonnaise if the dip is too dense; mix until smooth or to your desired consistency. Serve with a grilled garlic baguette and cold beer, if desired. The dip will keep in an airtight container in the refrigerator up to 1 week.

CHAMPIONS CORNER

For a smoother pimento cheese dip, you can briefly pulse the mixture in a food processor. Pimento cheese is more versatile than you think. Try it melted on a burger for a Southern twist or stuffed into jalapeños and wrapped with bacon for an appetizer. This pimento cheese dip tastes better after a day in the refrigerator, as the flavors have more time to develop and meld together.

BACON POPCORN

SERVES 4

8 slices bacon

½ cup bacon grease

1¾ cups fresh corn kernels

1 tablespoon salt

We're going to take America's favorite movie time snack—popcorn—and bring a carnivorous twist to it by infusing it with the rich flavors of bacon. Whether you're making Bacon Popcorn for a night at home, or as a unique side dish at your next barbeque, this delightful and irresistible mixture of salty, savory, and crunchy goodness is a delicious way to bring more fun into popcorn making.

Add the bacon slices to a large skillet over medium heat. Cook the bacon until crispy. Remove the bacon and place on a cooling rack so the strips stay crispy. Note: For a barbeque flavor, season bacon with G-Que Barbeque The Rub (or your favorite barbeque rub) before cooking.

Add the bacon grease to a medium-large pot over medium-high heat. Note: Use the bacon grease from the skillet. If you need more to make up the ½ cup of grease, hopefully you have some reserved bacon grease on hand. I like to keep a can of bacon grease under my sink, which I continually add to when cooking bacon. Test the heat by adding one or two popcorn kernels to the pot. Once they pop, add the rest of the popcorn kernels and cover with a lid or a sheet of aluminum foil.

Gently shake the pot back and forth over the burner. Once the popping slows down to about 2 seconds between pops, remove the pot from the heat. Keep the lid on for an additional minute to allow any final kernels to pop.

Transfer the popped popcorn to a large mixing bowl. Salt the popcorn while still hot. Break up the bacon into crispy bacon bits and add to the bowl. Toss well to distribute the bacon and salt evenly and serve warm.

CHAMPIONS CORNER

Depending on the palate of those enjoying the Bacon Popcorn, feel free to add ⅓ cup of Parmesan cheese and/or melted butter. This popcorn is best enjoyed immediately after preparation for the perfect blend of textures, from the crispiness of the bacon to the light crunch of the popcorn.

BACON ONION RINGS

SERVES 4 TO 6

- 2 large Vidalia onions, peeled
- 12 to 16 slices thin-cut bacon
- ½ cup G-Que Barbeque The Rub, or your favorite barbeque rub
- 1 cup G-Que Barbeque Hottish Sauce, or your favorite barbeque sauce

Thin-cut bacon is preferable as it wraps easily and cooks through without burning. Don't forget to give the strips a slight stretch before wrapping to make them more pliable and easier to handle when wrapping the rings.

Bacon-wrapped onion rings are a mouthwatering bite of savory and sweet, blending the smoky richness of bacon with the mild sweetness of onions. Each bite delivers a satisfying crunch from the crispy bacon exterior, giving way to the tender, flavorful onion inside. Whether served as an indulgent topping to a grilled burger, a decadent starter for your friends and family to nibble on, or as a delightful side dish to your smoked brisket or ribs, these Bacon Onion Rings are sure to steal the spotlight at your next gathering.

Preheat your smoker to 300°F using any smoking wood available to you.

Cut the onions into 1/2-inch-thick rings. Be careful when separating the rings. Next, take a slice of bacon and tug on it. This will help make it more pliable and easier to handle when wrapping the rings. Wrap each onion ring with a slice or two of bacon, overlapping the bacon slightly to cover the onion completely. For the smaller rings, cut the bacon in half lengthwise, which will allow you to get those smaller slices of onion wrapped easier. Secure the ends with a toothpick, if necessary.

Season around the bacon-wrapped onion ring with a medium coat of barbeque rub. Then place the onion rings on the smoker, close the lid, and let smoke for 20 to 30 minutes, turning halfway through, until the bacon is crispy and golden. Brush both sides of the onion rings during the last 7 minutes of cooking with the barbeque sauce. This will give the rings nice flavor and color. Remove the onion rings when the bacon is cooked through. Serve immediately while the bacon is crispy.

PORK BELLY BURNT ENDS
("BACON-WRAPPED BACON")

SERVES 6 TO 8

- 1 (5-pound) slab pork belly, cut into 1½-inch cubes
- G-Que Barbeque The Rub, or your favorite barbeque rub, as needed
- 2½ cups G-Que Barbeque Hottish Sauce, or your favorite hot barbeque sauce, divided
- ½ cup light beer
- ½ cup peach preserves
- 2 tablespoons high-quality bourbon
- 1 package (12 to 16 slices) bacon

Ready for some bacon wrapped bacon? We are going to cube pork belly into chunks, smoke them, then wrap them in bacon and glaze to create one of the most heavenly bites in all of barbeque. At G-Que Barbeque, we'll make this dish without the bacon wrap and serve as one of our most popular specials. Prepare your senses for an experience that elevates the humble pork belly into a work of art. Each bite is a morsel of perfection, lovingly bathed in a bourbon glaze.

Prepare a smoker to 275°F using hickory.

Season the pork belly cubes on all sides with the barbeque rub. Arrange on a baker's rack and place in the smoker until the internal temperature of the bellies reach 180°F. Remove from the smoker and set aside.

Lay down a large sheet of heavy-duty aluminum foil. Add the pork bellies to the center of the foil, along with ½ cup of the hot barbeque sauce and the beer. Tightly wrap in the foil. Note: The tighter the wrap, the more tender the bellies. Return to the smoker and cook for 75 to 90 minutes, or until the bellies are fall-apart tender with an internal temperature of 205°F. Remove from the smoker and set aside.

To make the glaze, add the remaining hot barbeque sauce to a saucepan along with the peach preserves and bourbon. Mix until combined. Place in the smoker for 20 minutes.

Season the bacon with the barbeque rub and place on the smoker alongside the glaze. Smoke for 15 minutes. Note: The bacon should be partially cooked and still pliable. Remove

the bacon and set aside. Remove the glaze 5 minutes later and set aside as well.

Take one end of a bacon strip and wrap around a reserved pork belly cube bringing the strip to overlap the other end of bacon. This will leave two sides without bacon coverage. Repeat with the remaining bacon slices and pork bellies. Dip each bacon-wrapped belly into the reserved glaze and arrange on a baker's rack. Return to the smoker and smoke for 15 minutes to allow the sauce to set up into the pork belly and allow the bacon to fuse together. Remove from the smoker and serve.

CHAMPIONS CORNER

When purchasing pork belly, observe how much fat there is. Thin striations of fat are going to melt during the cooking process and contribute significant amounts of flavor to the pork. This cut comes from the belly of the pig and is made from layers of fat and meat. Pork belly is the same cut of meat bacon is made from. Pork belly is unique because it's really the only protein on a pig that can be cut into bites and smoked.

CHAMPIONSHIP BBQ

BEER CHILI IN A BACON BOWL

SERVES 7 TO 9

Bacon Bowl

Makes 1 bowl (increase recipe for additional Bacon Bowls)

12 to 16 slices thick-cut bacon (number of strips depends on the bowl size)

1 tablespoon G-Que Barbeque The Rub, or your favorite barbeque rub

Beer Chili

¼ cup canola oil

1 yellow onion, peeled and finely chopped

3 to 5 jalapeños, finely chopped

¼ cup G-Que Barbeque The Rub, or your favorite barbeque rub, divided

2 pounds 80/20 ground beef

2 cups low sodium beef broth

1 cup tomato sauce

1 teaspoon paprika

5 tablespoons chili powder

1 tablespoon ground cumin

1 teaspoon garlic powder

½ teaspoon cayenne pepper

1 (15.5 ounce) can pinto beans

1 (12 ounce) bottle beer (Seasonal Oktoberfest)

Kosher salt and fresh cracked black pepper, to taste

Garnishes: Shredded cheese, sour cream, smoked bacon bits, sliced jalapeños

Tailgate chili is more than just a dish, it's a tradition that brings friends and family together in the spirit of camaraderie and competition. I have tasted and perfected countless chili recipes over the years. In fact, my chili recipes are the most viewed on YouTube. This tailgate chili is the culmination of those experiences, blending complementary spices, and a rich, savory broth into a pot of pure comfort. Whether you're gathered around the grill at a football game or enjoying a cozy backyard cookout, this chili will be the star of your tailgate menu, warming hearts and satisfying appetites with every spoonful. When entertaining, I like to put the chili out along with a garnish bar so guests can add whatever they like to their chili.

Prepare a drum smoker with hickory wood.

To make the Bacon Bowl: Choose a small, ovensafe bowl (metal or glass) as the mold for your Bacon Bowl. Lightly coat the outside of the bowl with non-stick cooking spray or a bit of oil to prevent the bacon from sticking. Set aside.

On a cutting board, lay half of the bacon strips side by side vertically, slightly overlapping. Then weave the remaining strips horizontally over and under the vertical strips to form a lattice or weave pattern. Press the weave together slightly to ensure it holds.

Next, wrap the bacon weave around the bowl by gently lifting the bacon weave off the cutting board and draping it over the bowl, pressing down to conform the bacon around the sides. Trim any excess bacon and tuck the edges under the bottom of the bowl for a neater look. Season the Bacon with the G-Que Barbeque The Rub. Then wrap some butchers

twine around the bowl so the bacon holds its shape as it cooks.

To smoke the Bacon Bowl: Preheat the smoker to 350°F. Carefully place the bowl with the bacon weave into the smoker, weave-side up. Smoke for about 45 minutes to 1 hour, or until the bacon is crispy and has set into a bowl shape. Remove and let cool slightly, then gently lift the bacon bowl off the mold, using a spatula to help if needed. Allow the bacon to cool further to firm up its shape. Set aside.

To make the Beer Chili: Add the oil to a Dutch oven and place on the smoker. When the oil is heated, add the onions and jalapeños. Season with the barbeque rub. Cook until the vegetables are soft, and the onions are translucent, about 8 minutes. Add the ground beef and season with a little more barbeque rub. Note: Flatten the meat to maximize the surface area, which helps the smoke adhere better. Return the Dutch oven to the smoker for 15 to 20 minutes. Remove from the heat and drain any excess fat. Add the beef broth, tomato sauce, paprika, chili powder, cumin, garlic powder, and cayenne. Stir to combine, then add the beans and gently incorporate. Return to the smoker and let simmer for 35 to 40 minutes. Stir the chili mixture and continue to cook for another 20 minutes. Stir in the beer and cook for an additional 30 minutes, or until the chili achieves the consistency you prefer. Taste and season with salt and pepper, if necessary. Serve in a Bacon Bowl along with the assorted garnishments.

CHAMPIONS CORNER

When selecting beer for this chili, choose a beer that complements the rich flavors of the chili. A dark ale or stout will add depth of flavor, while a lighter beer might be less noticeable. I prefer a seasonal Oktoberfest brew. When adding the beer, you'll notice the chili will appear a bit soupy. Allow the chili to simmer uncovered to thicken. If the chili thickens too much, you can add a bit more beer until you achieve the consistency you prefer.

BRISKET QUESO

SERVES 10 TO 12

- 3 Jalapeño Cheddar Sausages (page 74)
- 2 tablespoons unsalted butter
- ½ white onion, peeled and diced
- Salt and fresh cracked black pepper, to taste
- 1 cup heavy whipping cream, plus more if needed
- 1¼ cups (10 ounces) cubed Velveeta cheese
- 1 cup (8 ounces) shredded pepper jack cheese
- 3 jalapeños, seeded and diced
- 3 Roma tomatoes, diced
- 1 pound lean cooked Beef Brisket (page 52)
- ⅓ cup (2½ ounces) G-Que Barbeque Hottish Sauce, or your favorite barbeque sauce
- ⅓ cup (2½ ounces) water
- 2 tablespoons, or to taste, G-Que Barbeque The Rub, or your favorite barbeque rub
- Pickled Red Onion (page 94), as needed, for garnish
- Sliced jalapeños, as needed, for garnish

My family loves the luscious and creamy concoction of warm, gooey queso and I enjoy making it for them. The trick to a terrific queso is the cheese. I like Velveeta. It's creamy, velvety smooth, and I find it melts perfectly for dipping. I'm sure some folks out there don't like the idea of using processed cheese. If you're one of those, feel free to substitute the Velveeta with any of your favorite cheeses. Just know you might not get the same smoothness when dipping. The other key ingredient in this rich, flavorful dip is the peppers. I prefer jalapeños because my wife and kids can tolerate them, especially with the seeds removed. The dairy from the cheese also helps cut the heat level. If you prefer a spicier queso when dipping and dunking, raise the Scoville scale with Scotch bonnet or habaneros.

Preheat an outdoor grill to medium heat.

When the grill is ready, add the Jalapeño Cheddar Sausages. Grill the sausages, turning occasionally, until they're plump and reach an internal temperature of 160°F. Remove the sausages from the heat and chop into small pieces. Set aside.

Add the butter to a cast-iron skillet or grill-proof pot and place on the grill. When the butter is melted, add the onions and season with salt and pepper. Grill the onions, stirring occasionally, until they're lightly browned and translucent, about 5 to 7 minutes. Add the heavy whipping cream and cook for 1 minute. Add the Velveeta and shredded pepper jack. Cook until the cheese has melted down. Add the reserved Jalapeño Cheddar Sausages, jalapeños, and tomatoes. Whisk together and continue to cook.

Next, reheat the reserved brisket. To do so, place in foil and cover with the barbeque sauce and water. Wrap tightly in heavy-duty foil and double wrap to make sure the liquids don't leak through. Place on the grill.

The cheese has now been cooking for a few minutes. Whisk in the barbeque rub and continue to cook, stirring occasionally, for another 6 minutes. Note: If you find the queso is too thick, you can thin it out by adding more heavy cream.

Remove the warmed brisket and chop the meat, pouring the juices in the foil over the meat. Remove the melted cheese and divide into serving bowls. Top with the chopped brisket and garnish with the Pickled Red Onions and jalapeño slices. Serve with tortilla chips.

CHAMPIONS CORNER

The key to this mouthwatering queso is the layering of flavors. The inclusion of the smoked brisket adds a deep, smoky undertone that complements the spicy sausage to satisfy the carnivorous craving. For a smoother queso, you can blend the tomatoes, onions, and peppers before adding them to the cheese mixture. This recipe is versatile so feel free to adjust the level of spice to suit your individual taste by adding more or less peppers or different ingredients. The queso can be made a day ahead and reheated, making it perfect for entertaining.

STADIUM NACHOS

SERVES 3 TO 4

Corn Relish

2 cups fresh lime juice

¾ cup granulated sugar

½ tablespoon kosher salt

3 pounds fresh corn (about 6 cobs)

1 red bell pepper, diced

1 green bell pepper, diced

1 red onion, peeled and diced

Cheese Sauce

2½ cups freshly shredded mild cheddar cheese

1 tablespoon cornstarch

1 (12-ounce) can evaporated milk

1 tablespoon hot sauce, or to taste

1 teaspoon kosher salt

¼ cup G-Que Barbeque Hottish Sauce, or your favorite barbeque sauce

1 cup cooked Beef Brisket (page 52)

1 cup Easy Pulled Pork (page 70)

3 jalapeños

1-pound bag of your favorite tortilla chips

½ cup cotija cheese

½ cup sour cream, combined with 2 tablespoons water

We sell so many of these stadium nachos from our G-Que Barbeque stall at Denver's Empower Field and Folsom Field. During home Bronco games, we never stop making these. They're always a hit, and now you have our secret recipe. When making at home, you'll discover the Corn Relish makes much more than you need. Simply refrigerate the unused portion in an airtight container and use on other delicious items, such as tacos or quesadillas.

Prepare the grill for two-zone cooking (page 30).

Begin by making the Corn Relish: Add the lime juice, sugar, and salt to a large bowl. Stir until the sugar and salt are dissolved. Add the corn, bell peppers, and onion. Toss well to combine and taste. Adjust with more lime juice, if necessary. Store in the refrigerator until ready to use.

To make the Cheese Sauce: Add the cheese and cornstarch to a saucepan and mix to combine. Add the evaporated milk, hot sauce, and salt. Cook over medium heat (middle of the grill), whisking often, until the cheese is smooth and melted. Keep warm until ready to use.

Toss the brisket and pork with the barbeque sauce and ¼ cup water. Wrap the meat in aluminum foil and place over medium heat to warm.

Next, add the jalapeños to the grill over medium-high heat. Remove them after they have been charred. Remove the skins and dice the peppers. Set aside.

To assemble the nachos: Arrange the tortilla chips on a large platter. Pour the warm Cheese Sauce over the chips, then

repeat with another layer of chips and cheese. Top with the warmed brisket and pork and Corn Relish. Sprinkle with the diced jalapeños and cotija cheese. Drizzle the sour cream over the top and serve.

CHAMPIONS CORNER

Use high-quality tortilla chips that are sturdy enough to hold up under the weight of the toppings. Fresh made chips can elevate the dish significantly. Proper layering of the chips ensures every bite is packed with flavor. Feel free to customize your nachos with additional toppings like guacamole, pico de gallo, or black beans to add more variety and flavor.

ADIUM LOCATIONS INSIDE
T MILE HIGH AND FOLSOM FI
DRINKS
GQUE
CHAMPIONSHIP BBQ
HOME OF THE
COLORADO BUFFALOES

COLA-BRAISED MEATBALLS

SERVES 8 TO 10

- 2 pounds 75/25 ground chuck roast
- G-Que Barbeque The Rub, or your favorite barbeque rub, as needed
- 2 eggs
- 2 cups G-Que Barbeque Hottish Sauce, or your favorite barbeque sauce
- 1 cup Dr Pepper
- 1 tablespoon minced fresh curly parsley
- 1 (16-ounce) bag of pretzel sticks

Unlike many meatball recipes that add bread or breadcrumbs to fill or stretch out the meatball, these meatballs include just meat, eggs, and some barbeque rub. At home, I like to grind my own meat. If you don't have a grinder, have your butcher grind you a couple pounds of 75/25 chuck roast. These super moist, tender, and flavorful meatballs, with an added touch of sweetness from the Dr Pepper, are one of those perfect recipes during game days and get-togethers as you can make these ahead of time and don't have to hover over the smoker on the day of. That's because these meatballs hold well in the braising liquid, allowing your guests to graze throughout the day.

Prepare a drum smoker with charcoal and hickory to 275°F.

Add the ground chuck to a bowl and season with a light coat of the barbeque rub. Add the eggs and gently mix until incorporated. Note: If you'd like to increase the amount of meatballs you're making, use 1 egg for every pound of meat.

Roll the meat into small balls, and don't pack too tight or they will be very dense when cooked. You're after a soft, tender meatball. Lightly season again with a coat of the barbeque rub.

Transfer the meatballs to a foiled pan and place in the smoker. Smoke until the internal temperature of the meat reaches 140°F.

To make the braising liquid, add the barbeque sauce and Dr Pepper to a saucepot and whisk until combined. Place on the smoker until warm. Then pour the liquid over the meatballs until it covers the meatballs halfway. Continue to smoke until

the internal temperature of the meat reaches 165°F. Note: I like to spoon the liquid over the meatballs about every 5 minutes during the final cooking process. Remove the meatballs and place on a platter. Skewer each meatball with a pretzel stick for a handle, garnish with parsley, and serve.

CHAMPIONS CORNER

I love the sweetness the Dr Pepper adds to the braising liquid, but you can also use beer. The type of beer can greatly affect the flavor of the liquid. A dark beer like stout or porter will give a rich, deep flavor while a light beer will be less pronounced. If you would like to serve these meatballs as a meal instead of a starter or snack, serve the meatballs over mashed potatoes, polenta, or even inside a sub roll for a hearty meatball sandwich.

GARLIC-PARMESAN CHICKEN WINGS

SERVES 4 TO 5

3 pounds chicken wings (drumettes, flats, or combination of both)

1½ teaspoons kosher salt

½ teaspoon fresh cracked black pepper

1½ teaspoons garlic powder

½ cup G-Que Barbeque The Rub, or your favorite barbeque rub

Garlic Parmesan Sauce

Makes about 1¾ cups

10 large garlic cloves, peeled and minced

2 sticks (1 cup) unsalted butter

¼ cup G-Que Barbeque The Rub, or your favorite barbeque rub

½ cup aged (at least 2 years) Parmesan cheese wedge

1 tablespoon fresh curly parsley, finely minced

When it comes to chicken wings, I prefer crispy skin as opposed to rubbery. For this recipe, I'm going to use the two-zone cooking method (page 30) in which I grill the wings over indirect heat, then finish them over high (direct) heat to get that crispy skin without overcooking and drying out the wings. I'll then toss them in a delicious Garlic Parmesan Sauce and top with Parmesan cheese and parsley. When shopping for wings, you can buy drumettes, flats, or a combination of both. Also, make sure to select quality wings, preferably fresh, and wings that are thin-skinned and white as opposed to wings with thick, yellow skin.

Preheat a charcoal grill using lump charcoal and a chimney (page 37). Also, make sure the grill grates are very clean (page 36).

Season the chicken wings with salt, pepper, garlic powder, and barbeque rub, and mix well to combine everything. Place the wings on the preheated grill over indirect heat. Place the meaty ends of the drumettes, if using, closest to the fire and the flats behind the drumettes or farthest away from the fire. This will help the wings cook evenly. Cook the wings, turning occasionally, until the wings reach an internal temperature of 150°F to 155°F. Note: Monitor the chicken wings and flip when necessary to keep from burning. In addition, when placing the lid back on the grill, make sure the vent is farthest away from the hot coals and opened so the hot air will be forced over the wings. While the wings are cooking, top them with one more coat of the seasoning. This extra step will give the wings a beautiful color after they're cooked.

When the wings reach temperature, move the wings over the coals (direct heat) to crisp the skin. While the wings are

crisping (watch them and turn often so they don't burn), you can make the Garlic Parmesan Sauce. Place a saucepot on the indirect side of the grill. Add the garlic cloves, butter, and barbeque rub. Note: If needed, or to melt the butter quicker, place the pot over direct heat, but be careful not to burn the butter.

When the wings are crisp, transfer them to a large bowl. Pour the butter sauce over the wings, then add the Parmesan cheese and parsley. Toss until the wings are well coated.

Arrange the wings on a serving tray and add more Parmesan cheese and parsley for garnish.

CHAMPIONS CORNER

If you intend to cook the wings in the oven, coat the wings in baking powder and place in the refrigerator for 8 to 24 hours prior to cooking. The baking powder will draw the moisture from the skin, making the skin super crispy.

G-QUE
BARBEQUE
G-QUE BBQ
COLORADO'S ONLY CHAMPIONSHIP BBQ

NASHVILLE HOT GRILLED CHICKEN WINGS

SERVES 4

2 pounds thin, white-skinned drumettes and wings

Sea salt and fresh cracked black pepper, as needed

Slices of white bread, as needed

Bread and butter pickles, as needed

Nashville Hot Sauce

3 tablespoons cayenne pepper, or to taste

1 tablespoon packed dark brown sugar

½ teaspoon paprika

½ teaspoon garlic powder

¾ teaspoon sea salt

1 teaspoon fresh cracked black pepper

½ cup melted Crisco (or other lard)

Selecting the right chicken wings is important with this recipe. Use fresh, not frozen, chicken with thin, bright white skin (not thick and yellow) to ensure the skin crisps up nicely on the grill. Frozen wings can retain moisture, which will affect the texture when grilled.

Unleash the fiery spirit of Nashville with this Nashville Hot Grilled Chicken Wings recipe, a dish that promises to blaze a trail of flavor across your palate. These wings are not just a meal, they are a manifesto of heat and flavor, grilled to perfection and coated in a smoky, spicy glaze that captures the boldness of Southern cooking. Get ready to turn up the heat and enjoy a taste of Nashville's famously fiery cuisine.

Season the chicken with salt and pepper and refrigerate for 12 hours to allow the salt to fully penetrate the skin.

To make the Nashville Hot Sauce: Mix the cayenne pepper, brown sugar, paprika, garlic powder, salt, and pepper in a bowl. Add the melted lard. Whisk thoroughly and set aside. Preheat a Weber grill with hot coals to 375°F to 400°F and add a strip of hickory wood to infuse the chicken wings with a robust hickory smoke flavor (page 26).

Arrange the chicken on the grill, ensuring none of the pieces are stacked on top of each other; this spacing allows air to circulate and helps the skin get crispy. Position the fattier side toward the fire, with the bone side facing away. Cook for 20 to 25 minutes, or until the internal temperature of the chicken reaches 115°F, then flip and rotate the chicken to ensure even cooking. Continue cooking until the internal temperature of the chicken reaches 160°F. Move the wings to direct heat and sear over the hot coals for 15 to 20 seconds on each side to achieve a crispy exterior. Remove the chicken and toss in the Nashville Hot Sauce until coated thoroughly.

Serve by placing some white bread on a platter then place the chicken on top, allowing the bread to soak up the extra sauce (great bite by the way). Garnish with bread and butter pickles.

TORTILLA CHIP SMOKED CHICKEN FINGERS

SERVES 4 TO 6

Hot Ranch Dipping Sauce

Makes ¾ cup

¾ cup (6 ounces) ranch dressing

Cayenne pepper, as needed (however much you can handle)

2 sprigs fresh curly parsley, finely minced

Chicken Fingers

3 cups buttermilk, optional

4 cups all-purpose flour

G-Que Barbeque The Rub, or your favorite barbeque poultry rub, as needed

3 eggs, beaten

½ cup whole milk

1 (9.25-ounce) bag of Doritos

1 (2-pound) package chicken strips

Here's a new twist on the typical chicken finger dinner, which many kids enjoy, like mine. Instead of serving the same ol' chicken, coat the strips in your children's favorite chips and then smoke the chicken to achieve that one-of-a-kind smoky barbeque flavor. Because this recipe involves Doritos and breading, many kids will want to help in the kitchen. I mean, what kid wouldn't want to make and eat a fun finger food? I also recommend seasoning both the flour and chicken with barbeque rub. A lot of competition barbeque is about layering flavors, and I like to add flavor whenever I can. For the dipping sauce, I will add cayenne to wake up the dip, but some might think otherwise. At home, I make one dip without cayenne for my wife and kids, and the other with cayenne for myself.

To make the Hot Ranch Dipping Sauce: Add the ranch dressing and cayenne to a mixing bowl. Mix well until combined. Set aside until ready to serve. When ready, transfer the dip to a serving cup and garnish the center with the parsley.

Preheat your outdoor smoker using hickory and targeting a temperature of 350°F.

Set up a dredging station by filling one bowl with the flour. Season the flour with the barbeque rub. Add the eggs and milk to a second bowl and mix until combined. Open the Doritos bag to let the air out and then, using your hands and knuckles, crush the Doritos in the bag until coarse and pour into a third bowl. Note: If you want a finer grind, add the chips to a food processor and grind until fine. However, for maximum Dorito flavor, stick with the coarse grind.

Season the chicken strips with the barbeque rub. (Note: If you have the time, soak the chicken in buttermilk for 2 hours before seasoning with the rub.) Dredge the strips first in the flour, gently shaking off the excess flour. Fully submerge the strips in the egg wash and gently allow the excess egg mixture to drip back into the bowl. Finish by dredging the strips in the Doritos, making sure the strips are completely covered.

Transfer the chicken strips to a wire rack sprayed with canola oil and smoke in the preheated smoker until the internal temperature of the chicken reaches 180°F, about 15 minutes.

Remove the chicken strips from the smoker and let rest for 2 or 3 minutes. Serve hot with the Hot Ranch Dipping Sauce.

CHAMPIONS CORNER

Feel free to experiment with different chip flavors, such as Cool Ranch, Nacho Cheese, Funyuns, and Flamin' Hot Cheetos. This recipe can also be adapted for the oven if your smoker is not available. Simply bake the breaded chicken tenders at 400°F for 20 to 25 minutes, or until crispy and cooked through. For the egg wash, I'll add a touch of whole milk. I find it helps dilute the egg flavor while adding richness to the wash.

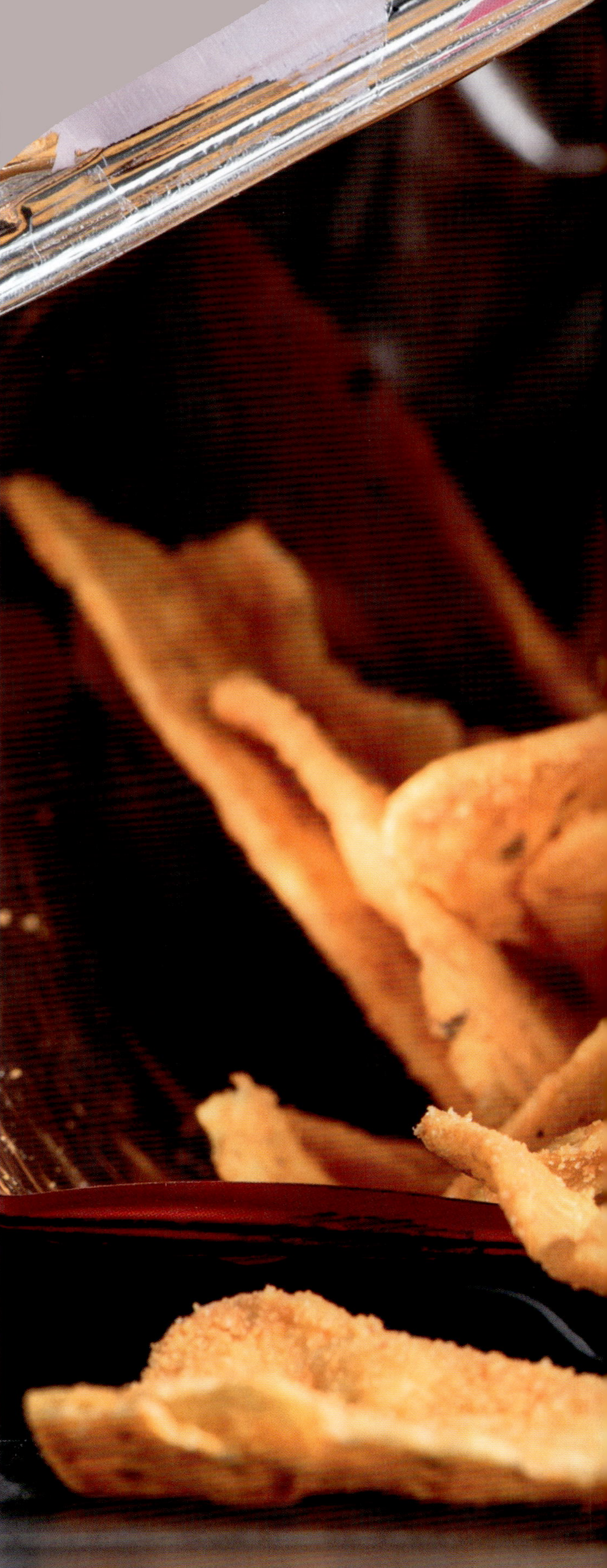

PRIME BEEF

Beef recipes have a way of capturing the essence of comfort, indulgence, and versatility. From the rich decadence of a perfectly cooked Tomahawk Steak with Roasted Garlic to the simplicity of Smoked Sloppy Joes, beef has the ability to fit any occasion and satisfy any craving. These recipes are more than just meals—they are experiences that bring people together, whether it's at a backyard barbeque, a family dinner, or a special celebration.

Some of my personal favorites are Smoked Sloppy Joes and Smoked Pot Roast. They take familiar comfort foods and elevate them with the deep, smoky flavor that only slow smoking can deliver. It's warm, hearty, and packed with flavor—pure comfort in every bite.

But beef doesn't stop at comfort food. This chapter also explores the luxurious side of beef, with recipes like filet mignon and tomahawk steaks that are fit for high-end dining. These cuts showcase the elegance and refinement that beef can bring to the table. Whether you're in the mood for something indulgent like Wagyu burgers or classic comfort like smoked pot roast, this chapter offers a wide range of recipes that highlight the versatility of beef. Each dish delivers big flavor, whether you're smoking, searing, or slow cooking. These recipes allow you to explore every aspect of what makes beef so special, from its rich marbling to its tender texture, creating meals that your family and guests will savor long after the plates are cleared.

BARBEQUE BRISKET LASAGNA

SERVES 12 TO 16

- ⅓ cup G-Que Original Barbeque Sauce, or your favorite barbeque sauce
- 1½ cups marinara sauce
- 2 pounds cooked prime beef brisket, finely chopped
- G-Que Barbeque The Rub, or your favorite barbeque rub, as needed
- 4 packages oven-ready lasagna noodles
- 32 slices mozzarella cheese
- 32 slices white American cheese
- 1 cup grated fresh Pecorino Romano
- 4 ounces (8 tablespoons) crushed red pepper, optional
- 1 bunch fresh curly parsley, stems removed, leaves finely chopped, for garnish

What should you do if you find yourself with leftover brisket? The answer is making a mouthwatering, meaty-cheesy barbequed brisket lasagna. This isn't just a dish, it's an event, a celebration of distinctly different flavors. When I first shared this recipe online, it got noticed by many national outlets. This lasagna is a unique twist on the classic, and one I find delicious.

Preheat the drum smoker to 325°F with hickory wood.

Add the barbeque sauce and marina sauce to a bowl and mix until combined. Set aside.

Add the chopped brisket to an aluminum pan and add a little sauce from the sauce bowl. Gently toss the meat until it's lightly coated with the sauce. Apply a light coating of barbeque rub and gently toss to incorporate. Place in the smoker and let warm until the meat reaches an internal temperature of 170°F. Note: We're not cooking the meat, it's already cooked. We're just warming.

While the meat is warming, prepare the lasagna. To a half-size foil pan add a layer of barbeque sauce to the bottom, making sure to coat the sides of the pan to prevent sticking. Place four sheets of the oven-ready noodles on top of the sauce. (Note: Do not overlap the noodles so they hold the shape of the lasagna. Also, keep in mind the noodles will expand as they cook.) Top the noodles with a layer of mozzarella cheese, followed by a layer of the warmed brisket, then a layer of the American cheese, and finally a layer of Pecorino Romano. Repeat the process with more layers until the pan is full, or you've used all the ingredients (you should end up with four or five layers. Don't use all the Pecorino Romano.

Save some for a final layer after the lasagna has cooked). Note: If you like a saucy lasagna, add a little more sauce on top of the brisket for each layer when building the lasagna. Finish with a layer of noodles on top and brush with a layer of the sauce. Place in the smoker, uncovered, and smoke until the noodles are cooked through, about 45 minutes.

Open the smoker and apply one final layer of Pecorino Romano to the top of the lasagna. Allow to smoke for another 5 minutes to get the cheese partially melted. Remove the lasagna and let it rest for 15 to 20 minutes. Note: Allowing the lasagna to rest is important. If you slice too early, the lasagna could fall apart and not hold its shape.

Cut the lasagna into squares, garnish with parsley, and serve.

CHAMPIONS CORNER

Feel free to experiment with different types of cheeses and the noodle-to-cheese ratio. For a meatier lasagna, increase the amount of meat mixture per layer.

BREAKFAST BRISKET TACOS

SERVES 10

10 slices bacon

G-Que Barbeque The Rub, or your favorite barbeque rub, as needed

1 tablespoon unsalted butter

10 large eggs

Kosher salt and fresh cracked black pepper, as needed

2½ pounds cooked Beef Brisket (page 52)

20 medium-size corn tortillas

1 cup Grilled Tomatillo Salsa (page 268)

½ cup shredded Monterey Jack cheese

½ cup shredded pepper jack cheese

Make sure you warm the tortillas before assembling the tacos. Warm tortillas are easier to work with and have a better flavor. These tacos are also very customizable. Add pickled jalapeños, sautéed onions, chorizo, beans, or whatever you like. Be adventurous.

I love breakfast and tacos. Naturally, a breakfast brisket taco seems to be the right choice here. And these tacos are amazingly delicious and a terrific use of leftover brisket and tomatillo salsa. Awaken your senses to the robust flavors of tender, slow-cooked brisket, fire roasted tomatillo salsa, fresh fried eggs, and crispy bacon. These tacos are perfect for a leisurely weekend breakfast or a decadent pre-tailgate meal.

Prepare a Blackstone Griddle or outdoor grill to medium heat.

Season the bacon with some barbeque rub and place on the griddle or in a cast-iron skillet over the heat. Cook until the bacon is crispy. Remove and transfer to a paper towel-lined plate to drain. To the griddle or skillet, add the butter. When melted, add the eggs and fry until sunny side up. Season the eggs with salt and pepper. While the eggs are frying, place the brisket and tortillas on the grill to warm.

To serve, place a fried egg on one of the warmed tortillas. Add a slice or two of brisket and a piece of bacon. Spoon a little Tomatillo Salsa over the top and sprinkle with the two cheeses. Repeat the process with the remaining tortillas and serve.

SMOKED BARBEQUE MEATLOAF

MAKES 5 TO 7 SERVINGS

- 1 small yellow onion, peeled and rough chopped
- 1 carrot, rough chopped
- 1 small red bell pepper, cored, seeded, and rough chopped
- 1 cup (9 ounces) Fresh Gourmet Cheese & Garlic Croutons, or another brand
- 2 pounds 80/20 ground beef
- 2 (4-ounce) pork sausage links (mild or spicy)
- G-Que Barbeque The Rub, or your favorite barbeque rub, as needed
- 1 large egg, beaten
- G-Que Barbeque Hottish Sauce, or your favorite barbeque sauce

If you're ready to try a delicious twist to the classic comfort food, smoke your meatloaf. I promise, you'll never go back to oven-made meatloaf again. That's because the infusion of smoke creates rich, smoky notes in the meat, enhancing the flavor while developing a moist, tender texture. For the breading, I prefer grinding cheese-and-garlic-flavored croutons. I've tried other variations, but these croutons really set this recipe apart from the competition.

Preheat the smoker to 350°F, using hickory. Note: You can also use oak or pecan.

Add the croutons to a blender or food processor and coarse-grind them. Remove the breadcrumbs and set aside.

Add the onion, carrot, and bell pepper to the blender or food processor and coarse grind. Note: Do not over blend and purée the vegetables. You want plenty of texture. Remove the vegetables and set aside.

Season the beef and sausage with the barbeque rub and add to a large mixing bowl. Add the reserved breadcrumbs, vegetables, and egg. Gently mix by hand, but do not over-mix. Form the loaf into a rectangle and transfer to a greased cooking rack placed inside a foil pan. Season the sides and top with a medium coat of the barbeque rub. This will help the loaf achieve good color and flavor as it cooks.

Place the meatloaf in the smoker and begin checking the temperature around the 45-minute mark (cooking times will vary). When the meatloaf reaches 150°F, add a light coat of the barbeque sauce and continue to cook the meatloaf until the internal temperature of the meat reaches 160°F in the

center. Note: It's okay to remove the meatloaf a little early from the smoker rather than a little late; don't risk drying out the meatloaf by over cooking.

Remove the meatloaf from the smoker and let rest for 8 to 10 minutes on a cooling rack before slicing.

CHAMPIONS CORNER

The key to making this a terrific meatloaf recipe is to not skimp on the fat. Because fat equals flavor and moisture, stay away from lean ground beef, like 90/10. Instead, choose fattier ground beef, such as 80/20. Also, do not cook the meatloaf beyond 160°F or you risk drying out the meat. For a twist on this dish, add a bacon weave and/or wrap the meatloaf in bacon prior to cooking.

SMOKED POT ROAST

MAKES 12 SERVINGS

1 (4-pound) well-marbled chuck roast

Salt and fresh cracked black pepper, as needed

G-Que Barbeque The Rub, or your favorite barbeque rub

1 yellow onion, peeled and coarsely chopped

1 head green cabbage, halved or quartered

6 large carrots, cut into 2-inch pieces

2 celery stalks, cut into 1-inch pieces

1 pound baby potatoes (or halved Yukon golds)

¾ cup (6 ounces) mushrooms

3 cloves garlic, peeled and finely chopped

1½ cups chicken broth

1½ cups beef broth

1 cup Malbec wine

1 sprig fresh rosemary

1 French baguette, optional

Here's an easy recipe for another classic comfort dish that delivers incredible results every time. The cooking process combines the smoker and the oven for exceptional aroma and flavor and plenty of melt-in-your-mouth tender beef. Cooking in one foil pan also eliminates a lot of clean up. When making pot roast, chuck roast is preferred. It's an inexpensive cut, and when cooked low and slow with aromatic vegetables, the roast transforms into a mouthwatering tender piece of beef with added depth from the braising liquid. One bite of this smoked pot roast and it will likely become your cozy Sunday go-to and a beloved cornerstone of your home cooking.

Preheat the drum smoker to 350°F, using charcoal and hickory.

Season the roast on all sides with salt, pepper, and the barbeque rub. Place the roast on a metal rack inside a foil pan. Transfer to the preheated smoker and smoke for 40 minutes. Turn the roast over on the rack to smoke for another 40 minutes. After about 80 minutes of smoking/cooking, a nice exterior crust should have developed on the meat. Internal temperature should also be 160°F. If not, keep cooking until the temperature is reached.

Preheat the oven to 350°F.

Remove the pan from the grill. Remove the grill rack and place the roast on the bottom of the pan. Arrange the onions, cabbage, carrots, celery, potatoes, and mushrooms, and garlic around the roast so the vegetables are evenly distributed. Add the chicken broth, beef broth, and wine. Note: The liquid should cover 50% of the roast. If it doesn't, add more liquid

using the ratio of 3 parts broth to 1 part wine. Place the rosemary on top of the roast and cover the pan with aluminum foil.

Place the pan in the preheated oven and roast for 3 hours or until the meat is fork tender and has reached an internal temperature of about 205°F. Remove the pan from the oven and let it rest, covered, for 10 to 15 minutes. Remove the foil and shred the meat with two forks. The shredded meat will begin absorbing the braising liquid.

Serve hot with the vegetables and a crispy French baguette for dipping and dunking.

CHAMPIONS CORNER

If you'd like to turn the braising liquid into a delicious gravy, add 2 tablespoons cornstarch and 2 tablespoons of cold water to a small bowl. Whisk until smooth. Remove the beef and vegetables from the pan and pour the liquid into a pot over medium-high heat. Bring to a boil and whisk in the cornstarch mixture, a little at a time, until thickened. Season with salt and pepper and serve.

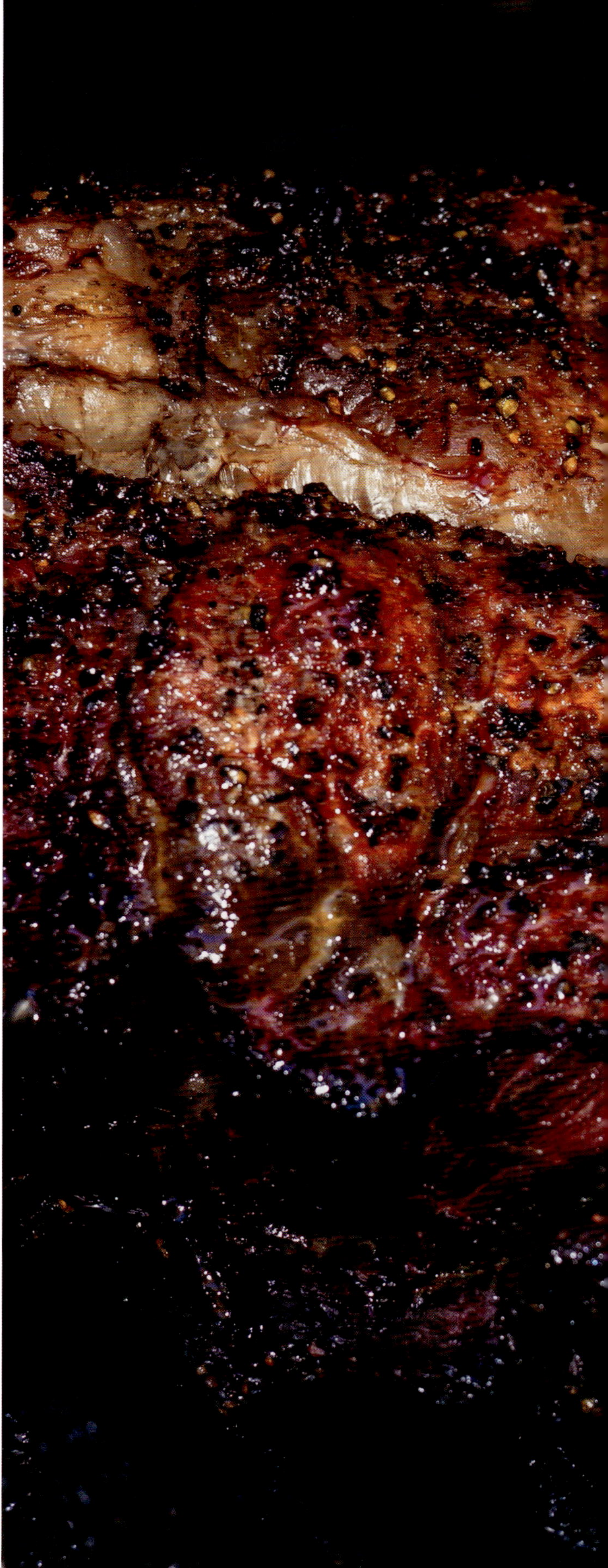

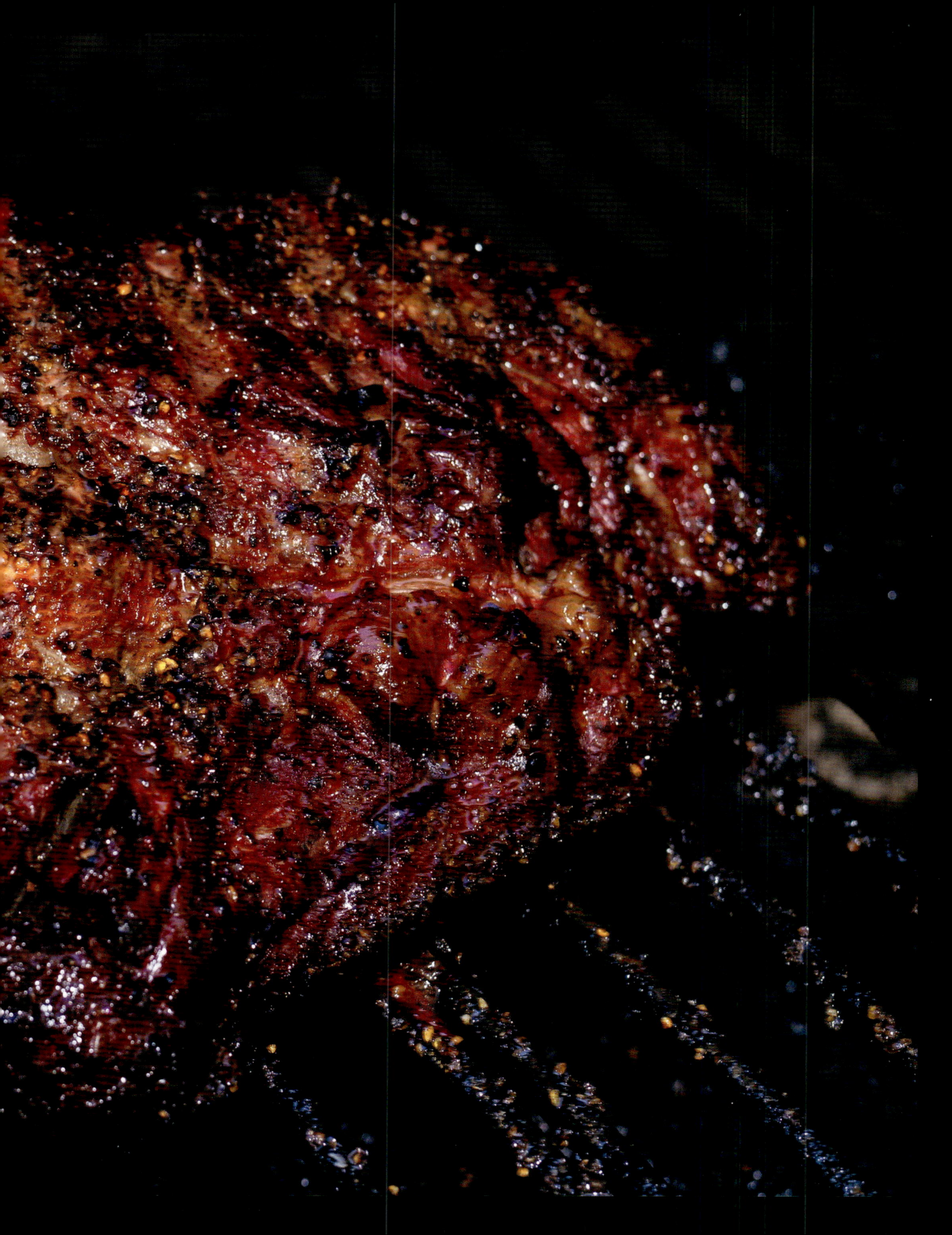

SMOKED SLOPPY JOES

MAKES 8 SERVINGS

- 2 pounds 80/20 ground beef
- Kosher salt and fresh cracked black pepper, as needed
- ½ red bell pepper, cored, seeded, and diced
- ½ green bell pepper, cored, seeded, and diced
- 1 small yellow onion, peeled and diced
- 2 cloves garlic, peeled and minced
- 8 Wonder Bread Classic Hamburger Buns (or brioche)
- 16 slices Kraft American Cheese (2 per sandwich)

Sloppy Joe Sauce

Makes just under 1¾ cups

- 1½ cups Heinz ketchup
- 2 teaspoons mild yellow mustard
- 2 tablespoons packed dark brown sugar
- ⅛ teaspoon cayenne pepper, optional

I've heard people say they don't like sloppy joes because they resemble a soggy sandwich. The secret to creating texture is buttering and grilling both the bottom and the top of the buns. This makes them less susceptible to absorbing excess moisture like a sponge while providing a pleasant contrast to the soft meat.

Bring a twist to classic sloppy joes by infusing them with smoky flavor. After trying this recipe, you will never cook sloppy joes in a skillet again. These sloppy joes are made in a drum smoker using hickory wood—perfect for barbequers looking to add a unique and flavorful option to their repertoire.

Add the beef to a foil pan and season with salt and pepper. Add the bell peppers, onion, and garlic. Mix to combine, then spread the meat in an even layer. Note: Spreading out the meat and maximizing the surface area will allow the meat to absorb more of the smokey flavor.

Add the ketchup, mustard, brown sugar, and cayenne, if using, to a bowl. Whisk together to make the sloppy joe sauce. Set aside.

Fill a basket halfway with coals and light. Once lit, set the basket in the drum smoker. Add a strip of hickory wood, and let the smoker heat to 300°F. Once at temperature, add the meat in the foil pan and cook to an internal temperature of 140°F, about 30 minutes. Remove the pan from the smoker, drain the grease out of the pan, and add the sauce along with ¾ cup of water. Mix well to combine.

Place the meat back into the smoker and cook for another 20 to 30 minutes, stirring halfway through. Note: This step is important to allow the flavors to come together and intensify.

Butter the buns and toast on the grill until lightly golden brown. Fill the buns with the sloppy joe mixture and top with two slices of cheese.

CHEESESTEAK BURGER WITH BOURBON CHEESE SAUCE

MAKES 3 BURGERS

¼ cup canola oil
1 large sweet yellow onion, peeled and thinly sliced
1 green bell pepper, thinly sliced
1 orange bell pepper, thinly sliced
1 jalapeño, sliced with seeds
G-Que Barbeque The Rub, or your favorite barbeque rub
½ cup high-quality bourbon
4 tablespoons unsalted butter, divided
2 tablespoons all-purpose flour
1¼ cups whole milk, warmed
1 cup shredded pepper jack cheese
1 cup shredded cheddar cheese
1 pound (80/20) ground beef
Kosher salt and fresh cracked black pepper, to taste
3 fresh hoagie or sub rolls

I love cheesesteaks, and we serve a mouthwatering brisket cheesesteak at G-Que Barbeque as one of our specials. If you don't have time to smoke a brisket at home, but would still like to savor that cheesesteak taste, try this recipe. What's really going to take this perfectly grilled burger over the top is the bourbon cheese sauce, which will give an opulent twist on the beloved classic. This creation blends the hearty allure of a traditional cheesesteak with the indulgent pleasure of a gourmet burger.

Preheat an outdoor PK grill with charcoal for two-zone cooking (page 30).

Add the oil to a large sauté pan and place on the indirect (low heat) side of the grill. When the oil is heated, add the onions, bell peppers, and jalapeño. Season with the barbeque rub and sauté the vegetables, stirring occasionally, until soft, about 6-8 minutes. Remove the pan from the grill, add the bourbon, and carefully light to ignite the alcohol. When the alcohol is cooked off (no more flame), return the pan to the indirect side of the grill. Add 2 tablespoons of the butter. When melted, add the flour and whisk continuously to achieve a golden-brown roux. Add the warm milk and whisk to incorporate. Add the cheeses and stir until combined with the vegetable mixture. Remove from the grill and set aside.

Loosely form the ground beef into elongated patties so they fit perfectly inside a hoagie or sub roll. Season both sides of the patties with salt and pepper and place on the indirect side of the grill. Cook the patties until they reach an internal temperature of about 130°F. Then move the patties to the direct (high heat) side to crisp them up.

While the burgers are cooking, melt the remaining 2 tablespoons of butter. Slice the hoagie rolls in half and remove some of the breading to make room for the burger and all the toppings. Brush the insides of the rolls with some of the melted butter and place on the grill to toast. Remove the rolls and set aside.

Baste the burgers with the remaining melted butter then remove from the grill. Place the patties in the toasted buns, top with the cheesy vegetable mixture, and serve.

CHAMPIONS CORNER

Use high-quality cheese as it melts better and provides superior flavor. Cheaper cheeses can often be oily or gritty. Always add the cheese over low heat to prevent the sauce from becoming grainy. The cheese should melt into the sauce gently for a smooth texture. Constant stirring while adding the cheese ensures an even melt and prevents any burning on the bottom of the pan. If the sauce thickens too much, add a splash of milk to bring back the creamy texture. Adjust the bourbon to taste but be mindful of its strength.

SMASHBURGER WITH BOURBON BACON JAM

MAKES 3 BURGERS

Bourbon Bacon Jam

Makes 12 tablespoons (4 tablespoons per burger)

- 1 pound thick-cut bacon, finely chopped
- 2 yellow onions, peeled and sliced
- ½ cup packed dark brown sugar
- 1 tablespoon balsamic vinegar
- 4 ounces high-quality bourbon

Smashburgers

- 1 pound (80/20) ground beef
- 1 tablespoon kosher salt
- 1 tablespoon fresh cracked black pepper
- 1 tablespoon G-Que Barbeque The Rub
- 2 tablespoons mayonnaise
- 1 tablespoon spicy brown deli mustard
- 1 teaspoon lemon juice
- 6 slices American cheese
- 3 hamburger buns, toasted
- 2 tablespoons butter or oil, for greasing

If you like juicy, seared beef patties smashed to crispy-edged perfection and crowned with a luscious, sweet, smoky bacon jam that will leave your taste buds dancing, this is your recipe. The beef patty develops that crispy, caramelized crust, which the smashburger is all about, while remaining juicy inside. Then the homemade Bourbon Bacon Jam is applied, adding a sweet, savory punch, with hints of smokiness from the bacon and subtle warmth from the bourbon. Every bite of this mouthwatering smashburger delivers a perfect balance of textures—crisp from the grill, soft from the bun, and rich with flavorful, decadent toppings. It's the ultimate burger experience.

To make the Bourbon Bacon Jam: Add the bacon to a medium skillet over medium heat. Cook until the bacon is brown and crispy, 10 to 15 minutes. Use a slotted spoon to transfer the bacon to a paper towel-lined plate, leaving the bacon fat in the skillet. Add the sliced onions. Cook over medium-high heat, stirring occasionally, until the onions are deeply caramelized, 15 to 20 minutes. Note: If the onions start to stick, add 1 tablespoon of water to help deglaze the pan. Add the brown sugar, reduce the heat to medium, continue to cook the onions for another 20 minutes or until completely caramelized. Add ½ cup of water along with the vinegar, bourbon, and cooked bacon. Bring the mixture to a simmer, then reduce the heat to low. Let the jam cook, uncovered, stirring occasionally, until the jam thickens and becomes syrupy, about 30 minutes. Once the jam has thickened, remove from the heat. Allow the jam to cool to room temperature, then transfer to an airtight container until ready to use. The jam can be stored in the refrigerator for up to 1 week.

To make the smashburgers: Preheat the outdoor griddle to medium-high heat. Loosely form the beef into roughly 2½-ounce meatballs. Add the salt, pepper, and G-Que Barbeque The Rub to a small bowl, mix to combine, and set aside. Add the mayonnaise, mustard, and lemon juice to another small bowl, mix to combine, and set aside.

Lightly grease the hot griddle with butter or oil. When heated, add the beef balls and using a sturdy spatula with a piece of parchment paper between the spatula and the beef, smash the balls down forming thin patties. Press and hold the spatula for 5 seconds. This will help the burger stick to the griddle, creating that beautiful smashburger crust. Season the burgers with the prepared seasoning. Grill the patties for 2 to 3 minutes on one side, or until the edges are crispy and the juices begin to rise to the top. Flip the patties and immediately place a slice of cheddar cheese on each patty. Cook for another 1 or 2 minutes, or until the cheese is melted and the burgers are cooked through.

To assemble, spread a generous amount of the prepared burger spread on the bottom halves of the toasted buns. Add 2 burger patties with the melted cheese onto the bottom bun. Add the Bacon Bourbon Jam on top of the burger patties and crown with the toasted bun on top and serve.

CHAMPIONS CORNER

Use high-quality ground beef and select an 80/20 blend for the perfect balance of flavor and juiciness. Make sure not to overwork the meat. Form loose balls to maintain tenderness and smash the burgers as soon as they hit the grill to get the desired crispy edges.

WAGYU BURGER WITH BEER CHEESE AND CRISPY BACON

MAKES 2 BURGERS

- 1 teaspoon kosher salt
- 1 teaspoon fresh cracked black pepper
- 1 teaspoon garlic powder
- 1 (16-ounce) bottle pilsner beer
- 1 cup cream cheese
- ½ pound jack cheese, freshly grated
- ½ pound cheddar cheese, freshly grated
- 2 tablespoons G-Que Barbeque The Rub, or your favorite barbeque rub
- 4 slices thick-cut bacon
- 1 pound Wagyu beef, formed into 2 (½-pound) patties
- 1 tablespoon unsalted butter
- 2 hamburger buns, toasted

If the beer cheese sauce gets too thick, add a splash more beer to reach your desired consistency. If the sauce is too thin, let it cook a bit longer to thicken.

Enjoying a homemade Wagyu burger with gooey beer cheese and crispy bacon is a decadence you must experience. The rich, buttery flavor of the Wagyu beef, known for its tenderness and marbling, creates a melt-in-your-mouth sensation. Each bite offers layers of flavor and texture, making this a truly luxurious, gourmet burger that satisfies on every level.

Prepare the grill for two-zone cooking (page 30).

Add the salt, pepper, and garlic powder to a small bowl and mix to combine. Set aside.

Add the beer to a heat-resistant saucepan and place on the grill over medium heat. Add the cream cheese and freshly shredded cheeses. Cook while whisking until the mixture is creamy, about 3-5 minutes. Season with the barbeque rub. About 1 tablespoon should do the trick. Set aside and keep warm.

Add the bacon to a cast-iron skillet over medium heat. Cook until the bacon is crispy then remove the bacon. Leave some of the bacon grease in the skillet and keep the skillet on the heat.

Lightly season the burgers with the prepared seasoning and add them to the cast-iron skillet. Baste the burgers while they're cooking with the rendered fat in the skillet. During the final minute of cooking, sprinkle the burgers with a little barbeque rub.

Assemble the burgers by placing the patties on the bottom buns and then drizzling some of the warm beer cheese over the burgers. Add the crispy bacon, crown the burgers with the top buns, and serve.

GRILLED PRIME FILET MIGNON

SERVES 4

- 4 (2-inch/12-ounce) prime filet mignons
- Sea salt and fresh cracked black pepper, as needed
- 1 stick (½ cup) unsalted butter

Grilled prime filet mignon on the barbeque delivers an unforgettable taste experience. The high-quality cut is naturally tender, and when seared on a hot grill, the outside forms a delicious, smoky crust, while maintaining a melt-in-your-mouth center, with savory, smoky notes that make it a true indulgence when prepared at home.

Prepare an outdoor grill for two-zone cooking (page 30).

Season all sides of the filets with salt and pepper. Place on the indirect (low heat) side of the grill and cook until they reach an internal temp of 100°F. While the steaks are cooking, melt the butter. When the steaks reach temperature, rotate them 180 degrees so they cook evenly. When they reach 115°F, begin basting with the melted butter.

When the steaks reach 120°F, move them to the direct (high heat) side of the grill. Flip the steaks about every 30 seconds. What we're doing here is searing the crust while not overcooking the meat. Continue to baste with butter. Continue flipping and basting on the hot side until the internal temperature of the steaks reach 129°F. Remove them from the grill and let the steaks rest for 3 minutes. The internal temperature should reach about 132°F for medium rare. Wrap the steaks in aluminum foil with a couple pats of butter and let them continue to rest for 10 minutes.

After 10 minutes, remove the steaks from the foil, cut into slices, and pour the remaining melted butter and beef drippings collected from the foil over the slices. Season with additional salt, if necessary, and serve.

SLOW-SMOKED PRIME RIB WITH WHISKEY-PEPPERCORN SAUCE

SERVES 5 TO 6

Whiskey-Peppercorn Sauce

4 ounces high-quality whiskey

½ stick unsalted butter

1 tablespoon Dijon mustard

1 beef bouillon cube, crushed

1 tablespoon heavy whipping cream

½ tablespoon whole three-peppercorn blend (black, green, and red)

1 (6-pound) bone-in USDA Prime prime rib roast, trimmed of any excess fat

2 tablespoons kosher salt

2 tablespoons G-Que Barbeque The Rub, or your favorite barbeque rub

CHAMPIONS CORNER

It's important to maintain a consistent temperature in the smoker. Avoid opening the smoker frequently as this can lead to heat loss and an extended cooking time.

Welcome to a world of deep, decadent flavors with this recipe, courtesy of Jared Neumann, one of my chefs. Enjoy this mouthwatering dish anytime you're craving a beautiful piece of meat.

To make the Whiskey-Peppercorn Sauce: Add the whiskey to a sauce pot over medium-high heat. Once the alcohol has burned off, 6-8 minutes, add the butter. When the butter is melted, add the Dijon and crushed bouillon cube. Whisk to combine, then reduce the heat to the lowest setting. Finish by stirring in the heavy whipping cream and the peppercorns. Keep warm until ready to serve.

Preheat the smoker to 225°F using hickory wood (page 26). Lightly season the prime rib with kosher salt and let the meat rest for 30 minutes, up to 2 hours. Then lightly apply the barbeque rub over the entire rib.

Add the prime rib to the smoker and cook until the internal temperature in the middle of the roast reaches 125°F. About 15 minutes before the roast reaches temperature, preheat a barbeque or gas grill to high heat.

Remove the roast and transfer to the preheated grill or oven and sear until the edges of the roast are crispy, about 5 minutes. Note: At this point the internal temperature in the middle of the roast should register 130°F. Remove the roast and let rest for 15 minutes while lightly tenting the meat with foil so some air can escape.

To serve, carve the prime rib to your desired thickness and drizzle the Whiskey-Peppercorn Sauce over the top.

TOMAHAWK STEAK WITH ROASTED GARLIC

SERVES 2

1 (2-pound, 2- to 3-inch thick) prime tomahawk steak with exposed bone

½ cup kosher salt, plus more to season garlic

⅓ cup fresh cracked black pepper, plus more to season garlic

8 bulbs garlic

1 tablespoon G-Que Barbeque The Rub, or your favorite barbeque rub, divided

½ cup olive oil

10 sprigs fresh thyme, minced

¼ cup Montreal steak seasoning

1 teaspoon garlic powder

1 stick unsalted butter

¼ cup Maldon flake salt, optional

CHAMPIONS CORNER

Choose a high-quality tomahawk steak with rich marbling for tenderness and flavor. Though expensive, prime grade cuts are worth every penny, ensuring a memorable, restaurant-quality result at home.

The tomahawk steak is every steak lover's dream. This tomahawk's never going to get confused with the petite filet. I like a nice thick tomahawk, ideally 3 inches. You will surely overpay for this thick cut and long French bone at a steakhouse, so source your tomahawk from your favorite butcher or meat market and cook at home. The tomahawk, if you're not familiar, is essentially a rib eye that is attached to the bone on the top. Prepared with roasted garlic, it is one of my favorite bites in this book.

Season the steak on all sides with salt and pepper and let rest at room temperature for 30 minutes.

Preheat the indoor oven to 400°F.

To make the roasted garlic, cut the top of each bulb, removing about ¼-inch. Place the bulbs, with the uncut part down, in a muffin tin (to hold the bulbs in place). Drizzle the olive oil over the exposed tops, then season with some salt, pepper, ½ tablespoon of barbeque rub, and thyme. Cover the tin with foil and roast in the oven for 40 to 45 minutes, or until the garlic is very soft. Note: Given the enormous size of the steak, there likely won't be room on the grill to also roast the garlic. If you do have room, feel free to roast on the grill.

Prepare the grill for two-zone cooking (page 30).

After the tomahawk has been sitting for about 30 minutes, season with the Montreal steak seasoning and garlic powder. Add the steak to the indirect (low heat) side of the grill with the exposed bone over the direct (high heat) side. Note: Because the bone is exposed to high heat, allow the bone to

get some color, but then wrap in foil to avoid burning the bone or getting too dark. Cook the steak, turning after every 8 minutes, until the internal temperature reaches 115°F.

While the steak is cooking, make the steak butter. Remove the garlic from the oven and, using the side of a large knife, squeeze out the softened roasted garlic cloves from the bulbs. Then smash the garlic cloves together to form a paste (you'll need ⅓ cup for the steak butter). Add the garlic to a heat-resistant pot along with the butter and the remaining ½ tablespoon of barbeque rub and place over direct heat. Allow to melt, stirring occasionally.

Brush the garlic butter on both sides of the steak. Then transfer the steak to the direct side of the grill to sear. While the steak is searing, continue to baste the steak with the steak butter. Note: The butter will create flames, which is okay as this will ensure a delicious crust. Be careful not to burn the steak by flipping the steak every 30 seconds while searing. Remove from the grill when the internal temperature of the steak reaches about 130°F for medium rare. Note: Use a meat thermometer to check the internal temperature. This ensures you cook the steak to your preferred level of doneness without guessing.

While the steak rests, baste with more steak butter. Then slice the steak, sprinkle a little flake salt over the slices, and serve with a side of steak butter, and any leftover roasted garlic.

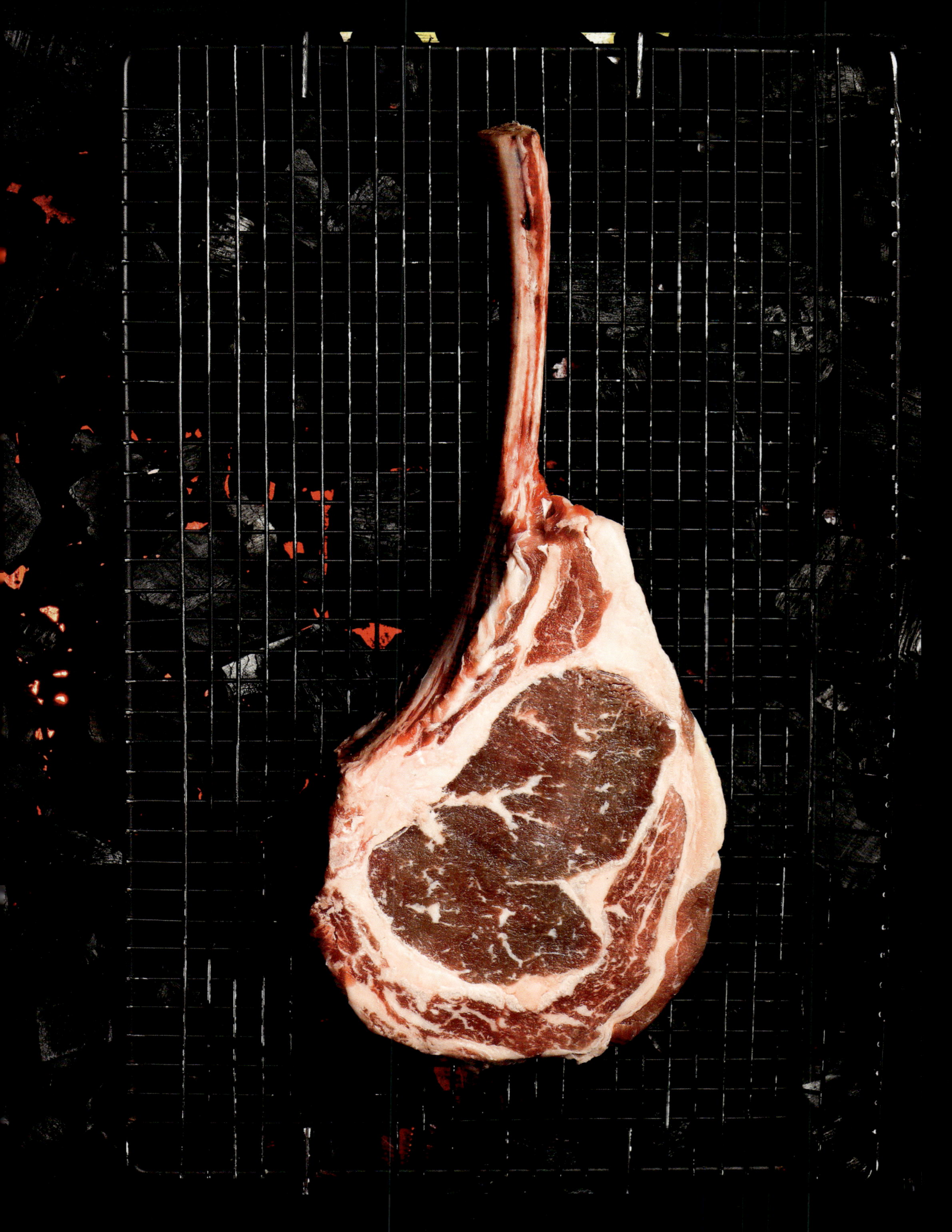

Finest Hogs

Pork has always been a cornerstone of barbeque and grilling, offering a wide range of flavors, textures, and cooking techniques. Whether it's the smoky, succulent layers of Cuban Mojo Pork or the sweet tang of Glazed Pork Tenderloin Braid with Apricot Barbeque Sauce, pork delivers a versatility that few other meats can match. For me, pork is about exploring bold flavors and trying new things, from traditional smoked cuts to more inventive dishes like the BLT Roll, which brings the familiar flavors of a classic sandwich together in a sushi-inspired presentation.

In this chapter, you'll discover a diverse collection of pork recipes, each designed to highlight the rich, savory qualities that make pork so beloved in barbeque. We'll go from grilling a perfect porterhouse with Dijon cream sauce to crafting Maple-Apple-Cranbery Pork Tenderloin that's both sweet and savory. You'll also find crowd-pleasing dishes like Grilled Jalapeño Cheddar Sausage with Peppers—perfect for any gathering. These recipes are meant to showcase the flexibility of pork, whether it's for a simple weeknight dinner or an impressive centerpiece for a special occasion. Through smoking, grilling, and creative flavor combinations, this chapter will help you bring out the best in pork with dishes that will leave your guests eager for more.

BLT ROLL WITH LEMON WASABI DIPPING SAUCE

MAKES 1 ROLL

Lemon Wasabi Dipping Sauce

Makes 5 ounces

4 ounces mayonnaise

1 ounce (depending on your spice level) wasabi paste

Lemon juice, as needed

12 slices thick-cut bacon

G-Que Barbeque The Rub, as needed, or your favorite pork rub

Pure maple syrup, as needed

Mayonnaise, as needed

6 thin slices of ripe yet firm red tomato, seasoned with salt and fresh cracked black pepper

2 or 3 leaves of green leaf, butter, or Bibb lettuce

If you're ready for a non-traditional BLT without the bread, this recipe is for you. It's my twist on the classic sandwich. We roll up the savory ingredients like a sushi roll. This way, you get delicious BLT taste in every bite. The key to making the roll is paying close attention to cooking the bacon just right. If it's overcooked, the bacon will easily crumble and fall apart. If undercooked, the bacon will be tough and chewy.

To make the Lemon Wasabi Dipping Sauce: Add the mayonnaise, wasabi, and a squeeze of lemon juice to a bowl and mix well. Transfer to a ramekin and refrigerate until ready to serve.

Preheat your smoker or oven to 375°F. If using the smoker, use hickory.

Lay out a large sheet of parchment paper or wax paper on your workspace. Take 6 slices of bacon and lay them side-by-side on the parchment paper, touching but not overlapping. This will form the base of your weave. Next, fold back every other slice of bacon from the base halfway so they're half the length they originally were. Now take another slice of bacon (the 7th piece) and lay it perpendicular across the bacon slices that have not been folded back. Unfold the folded slices back over this new slice. You've now started your weave. Continue the weave, moving the slices that were left flat in the previous step. Fold these back over the slice you just added. Take an 8th piece of bacon and lay it across the folded back slices. Unfold the slices back into their original position, over the new piece of bacon, keeping all the slices as tight as possible. Continue this pattern, alternating which slices you fold back,

and adding a new slice of bacon each time. Remember, after adding a new slice, always fold back the original slices to lay over the top of the new one. This creates the "weave" effect. Once all 12 slices of bacon have been used and your weave is complete, gently press down on the weave to ensure all the pieces are touching and are nice and tight. Lastly, use scissors to trim any flaps of bacon that extend out from each edge. We want all the edges to be uniform, creating a perfect square.

Season the bacon weave with the barbeque rub. Note: The rub will give the bacon good flavor but also create a deeper color as the bacon cooks.

Carefully transfer the bacon weave to a metal rack placed inside a foil pan to catch the grease. Place in the preheated smoker or oven for 20 minutes. Remove and brush the top side of the bacon with maple syrup (this will eventually be the inside of the roll). Carefully turn the bacon over, place back on the rack, and cook for about another 5 to 10 minutes, keeping a close eye on the bacon at this point. You want the bacon cooked through and pliable, but not crisp or it will crumble when you try to roll it.

Remove the bacon weave and place, syrup side up, on a flat surface to cool slightly. Then brush the bacon with a thin layer of mayonnaise. Add the tomato slices and lettuce leaves. Using a sushi mat, slowly roll the mat and BLT roll tightly while applying gentle pressure. When finished, use a sharp knife to slice the roll. Serve with the Lemon Wasabi Dipping Sauce.

CHAMPIONS CORNER

Enhance the mayonnaise in the roll with additional flavors. Experiment with various herbs and spices to find what you like best with your bacon. For an attractive presentation, slice the roll and arrange on a platter with extra lettuce leaves and tomato slices around the edges. This not only looks great but hints at the fresh ingredients inside.

PROSCIUTTO MAC 'N' CHEESE BOWL

SERVES 6

- 12 thin slices prosciutto
- 2½ cups elbow macaroni
- 2 tablespoons unsalted butter
- 2 tablespoons all-purpose flour
- 2 cups whole milk
- 1 cup grated sharp cheddar cheese
- 1 cup grated gruyère cheese
- G-Que Barbeque The Rub, or your favorite barbeque rub, as needed
- Salt and fresh cracked black pepper, as needed
- ½ cup panko breadcrumbs
- 2 tablespoons chopped fresh curly parsley, for garnish

Before I competed on the national stage in barbeque, I was often a judge at various barbeque competitions. One valuable observation I picked up was judges liked the unexpected, that little wrinkle in an entry that reflected the thought or time the pitmaster put into their dish. When I started competing, many contestants submitted recipes for mac 'n' cheese. That's when I decided to offer a luxurious twist on the classic comfort food by serving my mac 'n' cheese in an edible prosciutto bowl. The salty richness of the bowl complemented the creamy cheesiness of the macaroni perfectly, elevating the humble dish to gourmet status. When I submitted this recipe in the "Anything Goes" category, the judges were impressed. That was the wrinkle that differentiated me and G-Que Barbeque from the other entries, and we won time and time again.

Preheat the grill to 375°F.

Spray a muffin tin lightly with some non-stick cooking spray. Cut the prosciutto slices in half and then into 2-inch strips. Lay the strips in the tin holes in a crisscross fashion so the bottom gets 5 layers of prosciutto. This will allow the prosciutto to hold the mac and cheese without it falling through. Also make sure the prosciutto pieces are slightly overlapping on the sides. This will create the "wall" around the tin holes as you layer the prosciutto to form the bowls. Slightly overlapping the slices will also help prevent the macaroni and cheese from leaking through.

Place the tin on the grill for 10-15 minutes, or until the prosciutto is crispy. Remove and let cool before gently removing the prosciutto bowls.

Next, cook the macaroni according to package instructions until al dente. Drain and set aside. Note: Cooking your pasta to al dente is important as the pasta will continue to cook with the cheese sauce and breadcrumbs.

Add the butter to a saucepan over medium heat. When melted, whisk in the flour until smooth. Cook for 1 to 2 minutes to remove the raw flour taste. Gradually add the milk, whisking continuously, until the mixture is smooth and begins to thicken. Reduce the heat and add the cheeses, stirring until the cheeses are completely melted and the sauce is smooth. Season with the barbeque rub, salt, and pepper. Note: For a smooth cheese sauce, add the milk slowly and stir continuously to avoid lumps. If the sauce thickens too much, thin it out with additional milk until you achieve the desired consistency.

Add the cooked macaroni to the cheese sauce, stirring until well coated. Then spoon the macaroni and cheese into the crispy prosciutto bowls.

Finally, add the breadcrumbs on top of each macaroni-filled prosciutto bowl. Sprinkle some barbeque rub over the top, arrange the bowls on a baking sheet, and place under a broiler for 2 to 3 minutes, or until the breadcrumbs are golden and crispy. Remove from the oven, garnish with chopped parsley, and serve.

CHAMPIONS CORNER

Feel free to experiment with different cheeses, such as smoked gouda or fontina, for unique mac 'n' cheese flavors. Adding a little mustard powder or a few dashes of hot sauce also enhances the cheese sauce with another extra layer of flavor.

CUBAN MOJO PORK

SERVES 10 TO 12

Sour Orange Juice

1 cup fresh squeezed orange juice (about 3 oranges)

½ cup fresh squeezed lime juice (about 3 limes)

½ cup fresh squeezed lemon juice (about 2 lemons)

20 garlic cloves, peeled

1 teaspoon dried oregano

1 teaspoon cumin

1 teaspoon salt, plus more for seasoning the pork

1 teaspoon fresh cracked black pepper

1 (7- to 9-pound) bone-in Boston pork butt

1 small yellow onion, peeled and finely chopped

Dive into the heart of Cuban cuisine with this authentic Cuban Mojo Pork recipe, a dish that promises to tantalize your taste buds with rich, citrus-soaked flavors while transporting you to the vibrant streets of Havana. Infused with fresh citrus, this recipe will kick up ordinary pulled pork. The leftovers are perfect to make Cuban sandwiches. I love to make this recipe for those who've never had mojo pork before. Serve with beans, rice, and plantains for a classic Cuban meal.

To make the Sour Orange Juice: Add the fresh squeezed juices to a bowl and mix to combine.

Add the garlic, oregano, cumin, 1 teaspoon salt, pepper, and Sour Orange Juice to a blender. Blend until smooth. Set aside.

Season the pork with salt and place in a large Ziploc bag. Reserve 1 cup of Sour Orange Juice mixture and add the remaining to the bag with the pork. Seal and refrigerate at least 8 hours, preferably overnight.

Preheat the smoker to 275°F using hickory.

Add the marinated pork and cook until the internal temperature of the pork reaches 160°F. Drizzle ½ cup of the reserved Sour Orange Juice mixture over the pork, then wrap it tightly in foil. Return the pork to the smoker and continue cooking until tender and the internal temperature of the pork reaches 200°F.

Remove the pork and let vent for 5 minutes, then remove the foil and reserve the drippings, wrap again, and let rest at room temperature for 30 minutes.

While the pork is resting, make the finishing sauce.

To make the finishing sauce: Add the onion to a saucepot over medium-high heat. Sauté until soft and add the remaining ½ cup of Sour Orange Juice mixture along with ½ cup of the pork drippings. Bring to a boil, then reduce the heat to low and let simmer.

Remove the pork from the foil and pull the meat apart in chunks. Add the chunks to the saucepot and let the pork absorb the liquid. Once absorbed, remove from the heat, and serve.

CHAMPIONS CORNER

For the best results, marinate the pork overnight. This not only enhances the flavor but also improves the texture of the meat, giving the acid from the juice time to break down and tenderize the pork.

CUBANO STUFFED PORK LOIN

SERVES 6 TO 8

- 1 (2½-pound) pork top loin roast, boneless
- G-Que Barbeque The Rub, or your favorite barbeque rub, as needed
- 1 cup Cackalacky Bold Gold Sauce, or your favorite mustard sauce plus more for drizzling
- 12 slices Swiss cheese
- 1 pound thinly sliced deli ham
- ½ cup dill pickle chips

This recipe is from my friend Chris Gentry who lives down in Florida. He showed me how he elevates the classic pork loin to new heights, infusing the meat with the vibrant, robust flavors of a traditional Cuban sandwich. Imagine succulent pork loin, butterflied and generously stuffed with juicy ham, tangy pickles, melted Swiss cheese, and a zesty mustard sauce. Each bite is a burst of deliciousness—a perfect harmony of savory and tangy. Here, we unravel the secrets to creating this show-stopping dish that promises to wow your family and friends, leaving them craving more.

Preheat the smoker to 300°F.

With a sharp knife, slice the loin down the middle, being careful not to cut all the way through. Then slice again on the left and right of the center cut, using the same motion and being careful not to cut all the way through. When you are finished, you should have the pork loin with 4 long, deep slices separating the meat.

Next, turn over the "flattened" loin, and with a sharp boning knife, remove as much silver skin and fatty tissue you can from the backside.

Turn the trimmed loin back over and cover with a large sheet of plastic wrap. Using a rubber mallet, pound the inside of the meat until thin and flat. Use your best judgment.

Apply the G-Que Barbeque The Rub to the inside of the meat in a thin, even layer, followed by the Cackalacky Bold Gold Sauce in a thin, even layer. Next, add 5 to 6 slices of Swiss cheese down the center, depending on how long the pork loin is. Top the cheese with half of the deli ham. Add another light coat of G-Que Barbeque The Rub on the ham to season, then top the ham with the dill pickle chips. Repeat the process with another layer of cheese, ham, and seasoning. Note: If you have extra pickles, you can add them here.

Tightly roll the pork loin so all the ingredients are on the inside and then tie with butcher's twine to hold everything in place. Note: To help when tying, make a loop at one end of the twine, then pull the rest of the twine through. This will give a starting point when you wrap the pork loin. Take the string and slide it right underneath the end of the pork loin and go all the way down the loin and tie the twine at the end. Lightly season the outside of the pork loin with the G-Que Barbeque The Rub.

Place the loin on the smoker and smoke until the internal temperature of the loin reaches about 145°F, approximately 1 to 1½ hours. Remove the loin and let the meat rest for 2 minutes before removing the twine and slicing into 1- to 2-inch servings. Arrange the slices on a platter, drizzle some of the Cackalacky Bold Gold Mustard Sauce over the top, and serve.

CHAMPIONS CORNER

When the pork loin is finished, if you prefer that the cheese is not so oozy and liquidy, allow the loin to rest longer, up to 10 minutes, before slicing.

GLAZED PORK TENDERLOIN BRAID WITH APRICOT BARBEQUE SAUCE

SERVES 6 TO 8

- 1 (2-pound) pork tenderloin, trimmed with silver skin removed
- 6 tablespoons G-Que Barbeque The Rub, or your favorite barbeque rub
- 1 cup G-Que Barbeque Hottish Sauce, or your favorite hot barbeque sauce
- 3 tablespoons apple juice, divided
- ¼ cup apricot preserves
- 1 teaspoon apple cider vinegar

To ensure even cooking, try to braid the tenderloins as uniformly as possible. This helps maintain a consistent thickness throughout the braid.

Why serve a regular pork tenderloin when you can have a braided pork tenderloin? Braiding creates a unique presentation and culinary "twist" on the traditional pork tenderloin. This delicious loin features juicy, tender pork that's generously glazed with an apricot barbeque sauce, creating a perfect harmony of sweet and savory. Elevate your next dining experience with this fun twist on the classic.

Prepare the smoker to 325°F with hickory wood.

With a sharp knife, cut the tenderloin into three strips lengthwise, keeping about 1 inch at the end attached together.

Season each strip of pork with the barbeque rub. Note: Feel free to season each strip with a different barbeque rub if you have three different rubs available. Next, braid the loin by overlapping the strips like braiding one's hair. Use a toothpick, wood skewer, or butcher's twine to hold the loose end in place. Season the top and bottom sides of the loin with a light sprinkling of barbeque rub and place on the smoker. Cook until the internal temperature reaches 135°F.

While the pork loin is smoking, make the glaze. Add the barbeque sauce, apple juice, apricot preserves, and vinegar to a small saucepan. Mix until combined and the preserves have been absorbed. When your pork reaches an internal temperature of 130°F, brush the glaze on the pork and continue to cook the loin until it reaches an internal temperature of 145°F. Remove the loin from the grill and let cool for 2 or 3 minutes. Slice the loin, drizzle some remaining glaze over the top of the slices, and serve alongside a bed of Apple Slaw (page 90).

MAPLE-APPLE-CRANBERRY PORK TENDERLOIN

SERVES 6

Apple Maple Cranberry Sauce

Makes about 1½ cups

½ cup cranberry sauce

½ cup pure maple syrup

½ cup applesauce with cinnamon

1½ tablespoons Dijon mustard

1½ teaspoons salt

1½ teaspoons fresh cracked black pepper

2 (1-pound) pork tenderloins, trimmed

G-Que Barbeque The Rub, or your favorite barbeque rub, as needed

Look for pork tenderloins with a consistent thickness for even cooking. Avoid pre-marinated tenderloins, as they may contain additives which can impact the flavor or texture when smoked. Also, be sure to remove any silver skin from the tenderloin before seasoning. The tough connective tissue won't break down during cooking and can result in a chewy texture.

Here's a wonderful dish to enjoy during an autumn weekend of football or any festive gathering. The recipe is extremely easy, and the mouthwatering results will surprise your friends and family. That's because this pork tenderloin is smoked and basted in a mixture of maple syrup, apple, cranberry, mustard, and spices, infusing the meat with a rich, fruity essence reminiscent of fall. Smoking the tenderloin caramelizes the sauce, creating a flavorful crust while keeping the meat juicy and tender inside. The combination of maple sweetness, tart cranberries, and the natural savory profile of pork is how you'll want to prepare your next pork tenderloin.

To make the Apple Maple Cranberry Sauce: Add the cranberry sauce, maple syrup, applesauce, mustard, salt, and pepper to a saucepot over medium heat. Whisk until combined. Heat sauce for 10 minutes then remove from heat and keep warm until ready to use.

Preheat a smoker to 350°F using hickory wood.

Season the pork tenderloins with barbeque rub and place on the preheated smoker. Smoke until the internal temperature of the pork reaches 135°F, about 20 to 30 minutes. At this point, apply a layer of Apple Maple Cranberry Sauce to all sides of the loins. Continue to smoke the loins until they reach an internal temperature of 145°F, about 5 minutes. Remove the loins from the smoker and let them rest for 5 minutes before slicing them into medallions and serving the slices with extra Apple Maple Cranberry Sauce spooned over the top.

GRILLED PORTERHOUSE PORK CHOPS WITH DIJON CREAM

SERVES 4

Dijon Cream

Makes about 2½ cups

2 tablespoons salted butter

1 shallot, peeled and minced (about ¼ cup)

½ cup Pinot Grigio wine (or other dry wine)

¾ cup chicken stock

½ cup heavy cream

1 tablespoon Dijon mustard

¼ cup finely chopped fresh curly parsley

G-Que Barbeque The Rub, or your favorite barbeque rub, as needed

2 bone-in pork chops

Salt and fresh cracked black pepper, as needed

G-Que Barbeque The Rub, or your favorite barbeque rub, as needed

CHAMPIONS CORNER

When making at home, select the porterhouse pork chop. This cut combines both the tenderloin and the loin, resulting in a mouthwatering centerpiece of juicy perfection.

Pork chops are terrific for a weeknight dinner. They're inexpensive, quick and easy to make, and the succulent chops with their smoky flavor and tender texture pair well with most side dishes. If you're looking to elevate your traditional weeknight pork chop dinner, try this grilling recipe.

To make the Dijon Cream: Add the butter to a sauté pan over indirect heat. When the butter has melted, add the shallot and whisk to incorporate. Cook for 2 minutes, or until the shallot is soft, then add the wine, whisk, and bring to a boil. Add the chicken stock, whisk, and reduce by one-third. Add the cream, whisk, and reduce by half. Move the pan to the cool side of the grill and add the mustard and parsley, whisking thoroughly. Sprinkle in some of The Rub and whisk again to combine. Keep warm until ready to serve.

Start a chimney of lump charcoal and add the hot coals to one side of the grill (page 37). Add a chunk of hickory on top of the coals.

Lightly season one side of the pork chops with salt, pepper, and barbeque rub, then place the pork chops, seasoned side down, over indirect heat (275°F to 300°F). Season the top side with salt, pepper, and barbeque rub. Cook low and slow, rotating halfway through for even cooking, until the pork chops reach an internal temperature of 135°F, about 40 minutes. Move the pork chops over to direct heat and finish by regularly flipping them to make sure a crust develops on each side. Remove the pork chops when the internal temperature registers 145°F. Let the pork chops rest for 3 minutes. Drizzle the warm Dijon Cream over the pork chops and serve.

GRILLED JALAPEÑO CHEDDAR SAUSAGE AND PEPPERS

SERVES 8

1 green bell pepper, cored and sliced into strips

1 yellow or red pepper, cored and sliced into strips

1 yellow onion, peeled and sliced

2 tablespoons canola oil

Salt and fresh cracked black pepper, as needed

2 bottles beer

G-Que Barbeque The Rub, or your favorite barbeque rub

8 jalapeño cheddar sausage links

Spicy brown mustard, as needed, optional

Grilling sausages and vegetables not only impart a wonderful smoky flavor, but also simplifies cleanup. Keep a close eye on the meat and vegetables to prevent burning, especially the peppers and onions, which can char quickly. For the best flavor, select high-quality sausages from your local butcher or specialty store. If you're hosting a party or get-together, get a mix of sweet and spicy sausages to please various taste preferences.

When I'm having friends over for game day and I want to feed them, but don't want to spend a lot of time standing over the grill, this recipe is one of my favorites. That's because I can make these sausages ahead of time and then let them braise in the seasoned beer over low heat as the day goes along. By cooking the sausages in two stages—grilling first and finishing slowly in the beer braise—you get the delicious grill flavor without overcooking and drying out the sausage.

Set up the grill for two-zone cooking (page 30).

Brush the peppers and onions with the canola oil then season the vegetables with some salt and pepper. Arrange the vegetables on the grill over high (direct) heat until lightly charred. Remove the vegetables from the grill and transfer to a foiled pan. Add the beer and a light dusting of barbeque rub. Mix everything together and place on the low (indirect) side of the grill.

Add the sausages to the grill over high (direct) heat, and cook, turning occasionally, until they have some nice grill marks. (Note: You are not cooking them all the way through; you are just getting that grill color into the sausage before finishing them in the pan.) Add the sausages to the pan with the vegetables and beer and let sit over low heat until the sausages reach an internal temperature of 160°F.

Remove the sausage, peppers, and onions from the foil pan using a pair of tongs. The sausages can be enjoyed on their own, piled onto a grilled hoagie roll with some spicy mustard for a delicious sandwich, or served alongside other barbeque favorites for a complete meal.

All-Natural Birds

Poultry has always been a favorite when it comes to barbeque and grilling, and for good reason—it takes on smoky and grilled flavors beautifully. Whether it's the subtle infusion of smoke from a low-and-slow cook or the crispy, charred edges from high-heat grilling, poultry serves as a versatile canvas for flavor. Chicken, turkey, and even duck can absorb marinades and rubs well while remaining tender and juicy, making them ideal for experimentation with different cooking techniques and flavor profiles.

In this chapter, we explore a variety of recipes that highlight the versatility of poultry. You'll find bold flavors like the Honey-Lime Sriracha Grilled Chicken, which balances sweet and heat in perfect harmony, and the Grilled Chicken Teriyaki Pineapple Bowls, where the sweetness of the pineapple complements the savory teriyaki glaze. If you're feeling adventurous, the Bacon-Wrapped Duck adds a rich, indulgent twist to a classic favorite.

From lighter meals to hearty feasts, these poultry dishes showcase how well chicken, turkey, and duck can stand up to both smoke and fire. Whether you're grilling up a quick weeknight meal or planning a weekend barbeque, these recipes will help you bring out the best in all-natural birds, leaving your guests asking for more.

GRILLED CHICKEN TERIYAKI PINEAPPLE BOWLS

2 SERVINGS

6 boneless chicken thighs (1½ to 1¾ pounds)

1 (12-ounce) bottle spicy ginger teriyaki sauce

1 (4½-ounce) can coconut milk

1½ cups water

2 cups long grain white rice

⅛ teaspoon kosher salt

1 ripe pineapple

Sesame seeds, as needed

1 lime, cut in half

Drinking out of a pineapple is cool (page 122). You know what else is cool? Eating out of a pineapple. This delicious, aloha-inspired recipe—filled with juicy teriyaki chicken and fluffy white rice—allows you to serve your guests a mouthwatering dish inside a grilled pineapple bowl. When selecting pineapple at the grocery store or market, look for a golden yellow color at the bottom and sides of the pineapple. This will indicate ripeness. Gently squeeze the pineapple; it should yield slightly to pressure, but not be too soft. Smell the base; a sweet, fragrant aroma suggests ripeness. Lastly, check the leaves. If they tug out easily, the pineapple is likely ripe.

Add the chicken thighs to a bowl or Ziploc bag and add enough teriyaki sauce to liberally cover the chicken while reserving about ¾ cup sauce for later. Cover and let marinate in the refrigerator for at least 30 minutes.

Preheat a charcoal grill to medium high heat using hard lump charcoal and a chimney (page 37). Also, make sure the grill grates are very clean (page 36).

Begin by making the rice. Add the coconut milk and water to a foil pan and place on the preheated grill to liquefy the coconut milk. Once the coconut milk is completely melted, stir well to homogenize, then add the rice. Season with the salt. Cover the smoker with the lid. When the rice begins to boil, remove the pan from the smoker and cover with foil for 15 minutes while the rice finishes cooking.

While the rice finishes cooking, cut the pineapple directly in half—straight down the middle, lengthwise—then core

each half, leaving about ½ - 1 inch of pineapple flesh along the walls. Discard the inedible center, and finely chop the edible pineapple flesh and reserve.

Remove the chicken thighs from the marinade and place them on the preheated grill. Cook the chicken until the internal temperature reaches 165°F. While the chicken cooks, baste them with some of the extra teriyaki sauce while being sure to turn the chicken at least once. To ensure the chicken is juicy and not dried out, make sure not to cook the chicken beyond 185°F.

Remove the chicken and slice or chop into thin pieces. Place in a heat-proof pan along with the remaining teriyaki sauce. Next, place the pineapple halves face down on the grill just prior to serving to heat and get some fresh grill marks on the pineapple. Remove the pineapple and add a bed of rice in the bottom of the pineapple. Top with the caramelized chicken and reserved pineapple. Garnish with toasted sesame seeds, and half a lime.

CHAMPIONS CORNER

If you prefer to make your own teriyaki sauce rather than using store bought, here's a simple recipe for you. Mix 1½ tablespoons cornstarch with ¼ cup cold water to make a slurry. Next, add ¼ cup soy sauce, 1 cup water, ½ teaspoon ground ginger, ¼ teaspoon garlic powder, ⅓ cup packed brown sugar, ½ tablespoon honey, and a pinch of cayenne to a saucepan over medium heat. Bring to a simmer and add the slurry. Whisk until the mixture thickens to a teriyaki sauce consistency. If you prefer a thinner sauce, simply add some water.

HONEY-LIME SRIRACHA CHICKEN

MAKES 4 SERVINGS

12 fresh chicken drumsticks

4 tablespoons G-Que Barbeque The Rub, or your favorite barbeque rub

½ cup salted butter

½ cup sriracha

¾ cup Frank's RedHot Sauce

4 tablespoons fresh lime juice

4 tablespoons white vinegar

1¼ cups honey

Prepare to tantalize your taste buds with the ultimate wake up call to boring weeknight chicken. This mouthwatering recipe is a harmonious blend of sweet, tangy, and spicy flavors, promising a chicken experience like no other. Succulent chicken is sauced in a luscious concoction of golden honey, zesty lime, and fiery sriracha, then grilled to perfection, delivering a juicy, caramelized finish that will leave you craving more. Amp up your grilling game and impress your guests with this show-stopping dish that embodies the perfect balance of heat and sweetness.

Prepare an outdoor grill using two-zone cooking (page 30).

Season the chicken with the barbeque rub.

Add the butter, sriracha, Frank's RedHot Sauce, lime juice, vinegar, and honey to a small saucepot. Mix well and place over indirect (medium-low) heat and cook until homogenized, about 5 to 7 minutes. Keep warm until ready to use.

Place the meaty end of the drumsticks toward the direct (hot side) of the grill. Grill the chicken, rotating often for even cooking, until it reaches an internal temperature of 145°F. Be careful not to burn the chicken. Now move the chicken over direct heat while turning regularly to sear and crisp the skin. Do not burn and do not cook the chicken beyond an internal temperature of 170°F. Remove the chicken (ideally at 165°F) from the grill.

Coat the chicken liberally in the reserved sauce and return the chicken to the grill over indirect (medium) heat. Cook for 2 or 3 minutes, or until the sauce is set up. Remove the chicken, let cool for 2 minutes, and serve.

CHAMPIONS CORNER

To give more of a barbeque flavor to your chicken, add 1 cup of barbeque sauce to 1 cup of the Honey-Lime Sriracha Sauce.

SMOKED TURKEY BREAST

SERVES 5 TO 7

½ cup salted butter, softened

3 cloves garlic, peeled and minced

1 tablespoon G-Que Barbeque The Rub, or your favorite barbeque seasoning

1 (5- to 6-pound) fresh turkey breast, skin on

½ cup chicken broth

If you're looking for a tender, juicy turkey and aren't cooking for many people, this recipe is perfect for you. There's no basting or brining. Just a light, easy smoke. I prefer hickory and will add just one log to the smoker and burn it down for 15 to 20 minutes before adding the breast. The result is one of the most moist and delicious tasting turkeys you'll come across.

Preheat the smoker to 275°F.

Add the butter, garlic, and seasoning to a bowl. Mix well.

Pat the turkey breast dry with paper towels. Season with barbeque seasoning. Loosen the skin of the turkey breast and smear about a tablespoon of butter under the skin, then smear the remaining butter all over the outside of the breast. Place the breast in a baking dish and add the chicken broth. Transfer to the preheated smoker. Smoke until the internal temperature of the thickest part of the breast registers 155°F, about 1½ to 2½ hours. Remove the breast from the smoker and loosely tent with foil. Note: Yes, you can safely pull the turkey at 155°F and it will be safe and delicious to eat. Let the breast rest for 5 to 7 minutes before slicing and serving.

CHAMPIONS CORNER

Melt a little butter with the remaining pan juices and drizzle over the sliced breast before serving to maximize both the flavor and moisture of the meat.

BACON-WRAPPED DUCK WITH PINEAPPLE

SERVES 8 TO 10

- 2 pounds fresh duck breast, cut into bite-sized cubes
- G-Que Barbeque The Rub, or your favorite barbeque rub, as needed
- 1 (16-ounce) package bacon, cut into thirds
- 1 cup G-Que Barbeque Hottish Sauce, or your favorite barbeque sauce
- ¼ cup pineapple preserves
- 1 (20-ounce) can pineapple chunks

As with other proteins, try to avoid overcooking duck or the meat will be tough and chewy. Wrapping the duck in bacon and glazing helps protect the duck from being overcooked. You can also par cook the bacon for about 15 minutes before you wrap it around the duck, if desired.

I made these delicious bites in honor of my daughter Tori, who graduated from the University of Oregon. It's always fun to make food items representing the teams playing, and this easy recipe is something you should try at your next tailgate.

Prepare an outdoor smoker with fruit wood (apple or cherry) or hickory to 350°F (page 25).

Add the cubed duck breast to a bowl. Season with the barbeque rub. Gently toss to evenly coat. Then wrap each cube with a strip of bacon. Note: You should be able to get the bacon around the duck with about a ¼-inch overlap. If not, trim the bacon until you get that little overlap. Cooking with the overlap under the duck is important as this will fuse the bacon together during the cook.

Season the tops of the bacon-wrapped duck with a little more barbeque rub before placing into the preheated smoker. Smoke for about 35 minutes or until the bacon is cooked through and the internal temperature of the duck reaches at least 140°F.

While the duck is smoking, add the barbeque sauce to a saucepot along with the pineapple preserves. Mix well and heat the sauce in the smoker for 10 minutes.

Remove the duck and saucepot from the smoker. Dunk each bacon-wrapped duck bite into the warmed sauce and place back in the smoker for 10 minutes to let the sauce set. Remove from the smoker and serve each bite skewered with a pineapple chunk.

SUSTAINABLE SEAFOOD

Seafood and barbeque are a match made in heaven, and nothing showcases that better than the variety of recipes in this chapter. Whether it's the sweet and smoky flavor of Bourbon Bacon-Wrapped Shrimp or the rich, buttery taste of Beer Butter Scallops, grilling or smoking seafood takes it to another level. Cooking over fire brings out seafood's natural sweetness, adding depth and complexity to every bite that you just can't achieve in a kitchen. Seafood loves the grill, and the grill loves seafood right back.

One of the highlights of this chapter is the Grilled Lobster Tail, which happens to be the number one lobster tail video on YouTube. People can't get enough of the smoky, succulent lobster finished with seasoned garlic butter—it's pure indulgence.

In this chapter, you'll also find recipes like Tequila Lime Grilled Shrimp and Grilled King Crab Legs, each designed to elevate seafood's natural flavor with bold marinades and fresh ingredients. These dishes are not only delicious but also sustainable, allowing you to enjoy incredible flavors while respecting our oceans. Whether you're preparing the perfect Surf & Turf Smashburger or impressing guests with Honey-Garlic Grilled Shrimp, these seafood recipes are sure to satisfy.

BOURBON BACON-WRAPPED SHRIMP

SERVES 5 (2 SHRIMP PER SERVING)

If you're a fan of *Parks and Recreation*, you'll remember Ron Swanson's famous quote in which he shares that, "Bacon-wrapped shrimp is my number one favorite food wrapped around my number three favorite food." If Ron tried these bacon-wrapped shrimp with my bourbon glaze, I'm confident they would be his favorite recipe in the book. This recipe also happened to be my go-to during my barbeque competition days for the "Anything Goes" category. I would offer these succulent treats as a bonus to whatever else I was putting in the box. I consistently achieved the Top 3 in this category, winning a number of times thanks to the recipe below. I hope you enjoy them as much as the judges did.

Garlic Butter

Makes about ½ cup

1 stick salted butter

3 cloves garlic, peeled and smashed

Finely chopped fresh curly parsley, for garnish

Bourbon Glaze

¼ cup cocktail sauce (with horseradish)

1 cup G-Que Original Barbeque Sauce, or your favorite barbeque sauce

1½ ounces (3 tablespoons) Jim Beam Single Barrel Bourbon, or your favorite bourbon

1 lemon, optional

Other

10 (10/15) colossal raw shrimp, peeled, deveined, with tail attached

G-Que Barbeque The Rub, as needed

5 strips uncooked bacon, cut in half

To make the Garlic Butter: Add the butter, garlic, and parsley to a saucepan over medium heat. Cook, stirring often, until the butter is completely melted. Keep warm until ready to use.

To make the Bourbon Glaze: Add the cocktail sauce, barbeque sauce, and bourbon to a saucepan over medium heat. Cook, stirring often, until warm. Transfer to a preheated smoker for 2 minutes. Remove from the smoker, stir, and keep warm until ready to use.

Prepare a smoker to 350°F using hickory wood or pellets.

Coat each side of bacon with barbeque rub. Then wrap each piece of bacon around one shrimp and arrange in a foil pan with the shrimp standing upright with the tails facing up. Place in the smoker and smoke for 15 minutes. Note: The bacon should be 75% cooked at this point. Baste the shrimp heavily with Garlic Butter. Continue smoking the shrimp until

the bacon is cooked through, about another 8 minutes. Remove the shrimp and dunk each shrimp in the Bourbon Glaze. Return the shrimp to the smoker and continue smoking for 5 minutes. Remove the shrimp and baste again with the Garlic Butter. Arrange the shrimp on a serving platter, garnish with parsley, and squeeze a little lemon over the top, if desired. Let the shrimp rest for 2 minutes before serving.

CHAMPIONS CORNER

That final baste of Garlic Butter is a critical step to the smoking process. That's because you're layering the flavors—first Garlic Butter, then the Bourbon Glaze, then another layer of Garlic Butter. This adds a greater depth of flavor to the shrimp that would not be achieved if you added the butter and glaze all at once or didn't butter the shrimp again after the smoking process.

HONEY-GARLIC GRILLED SHRIMP

SERVES 3

⅓ cup low sodium soy sauce

⅓ cup honey

4 teaspoons fresh minced garlic

1 teaspoon grated fresh ginger

⅛ teaspoon cayenne pepper, or to your preference

1 tablespoon olive oil

12 (13/15) colossal raw shrimp, peeled, deveined, tail on

1 cup melted butter

Curley parsley, minced, as needed, for garnish

CHAMPIONS CORNER

The key to perfect grilled shrimp is not to overcook them. They should be opaque and slightly pink. Pay close attention to the grill, as the high sugar content in the honey can cause the shrimp to char quickly. The quality of shrimp is also important. Fresh, or properly thawed frozen, shrimp should be firm, clean-smelling, and bright in color. If they are not deveined and peeled, go-ahead and do that but leave the tail on. I find the tail acts as a "handle" for those like me who like to eat with their fingers.

If you're ready for some savory, sweet, belly-satisfying shrimp, you gotta try this recipe. When I was invited to cook at the Charleston Food and Wine festival, I prepared and served these Honey-Garlic Grilled Shrimp. The sweetness of the honey, the depth of the soy sauce, and the kick from the garlic and ginger take them over the top. I don't like to brag, but I had so many folks lining up two, three, even four times to enjoy these irresistible shrimp. At home, I'll serve them over a bed of rice, but they also make a great addition to grilled vegetables, salads, and pasta dishes.

Prepare the marinade by adding the soy sauce, honey, garlic, ginger, cayenne, and olive oil to a bowl. Mix well until combined. Reserve ⅓ of the marinade and pour the remaining into a one-gallon Ziploc bag. Add the shrimp to the bag and toss well. Remove as much air as you can from the bag, then seal the bag and place in the refrigerator for 25 minutes.

Start a chimney of lump charcoal and add the hot coals to one side of the grill (page 37).

Remove the shrimp from the bag and place on the cool side of the grill for 2 to 3 minutes. Then move the shrimp over to the hot side to get some good char marks and crispy edges. The shrimp are done when they turn orange, and the internal temperature reaches 125°F. Move the shrimp back to the cool side of the grill and brush with some of the melted butter. Let the shrimp sit in the low heat for 2 minutes, then remove from the heat and add them to a bowl and toss with the reserved marinade. Plate the shrimp, drizzle the remaining melted butter over the top, garnish with parsley, and serve.

TEQUILA LIME GRILLED SHRIMP

SERVES 6

- 1½ pounds (13/15) colossal raw shrimp, peeled, deveined, tail on
- ⅓ cup good-quality silver tequila, plus extra, if desired, to flambé
- ⅓ cup fresh lime juice (about 2 limes)
- ⅓ cup olive oil
- 3 tablespoons chopped fresh cilantro
- 2 garlic cloves, peeled and minced
- 1 teaspoon lime zest
- 1 teaspoon crushed red pepper flakes, or to taste
- 1 teaspoon honey
- Kosher salt and fresh cracked black pepper, to taste
- G-Que Barbeque The Rub, or your favorite barbeque rub, as needed
- Lime wedges and additional cilantro, for garnish

CHAMPIONS CORNER

Avoid marinating the shrimp for more than 30 minutes. Otherwise, the acid from the lime juice will begin to "cook" the shrimp and affect their texture. Always select large, fresh shrimp for the best flavor. Frozen shrimp can be used, but make sure the shrimp are completely thawed before marinating.

Tequila. Lime. Shrimp. Say no more. Succulent shrimp are marinated in a zesty blend of tequila, lime juice, cilantro, garlic, honey, and spices, then grilled to perfection. I like to serve this dish, which is always bursting with flavor, as an appetizer or main. If you prefer the shrimp as a main meal, serve them with my Bacon-Fried Corn (page 260). For the tequila, use whatever favorite tequila you have. My only advice is don't use a cheap inferior tequila. Cook with what you enjoy.

Add the tequila, lime juice, olive oil, cilantro, garlic, lime zest, red pepper flakes, and honey to a bowl. Mix well to combine, then season to taste with some salt, pepper, and barbeque rub. Add the contents to a large Ziploc bag, then add the shrimp and toss to coat evenly. Remove the air from the bag, seal, and refrigerate for 20 minutes.

Preheat the griddle to high heat.

Remove the shrimp from the marinade, letting any excess marinade drip off (discard the remaining marinade). Grill the shrimp for 2 to 3 minutes on each side, or until they are pink, opaque, and cooked through. If desired, add a splash of tequila over the shrimp, carefully light on fire, and flambé for 1 or 2 minutes. Remove the shrimp from the griddle, garnish with lime wedges and a sprinkle of fresh cilantro, and serve.

BEER BUTTER SCALLOPS

SERVES 2 (3 SCALLOPS PER PERSON)

- Vegetable oil, as needed
- 1 teaspoon sea salt
- 1 teaspoon fresh cracked black pepper
- 1 teaspoon G-Que Barbeque The Rub, or your favorite seafood rub
- 6 (U8-10) dry-packed sea scallops
- 2 tablespoons butter
- 1 lemon, cut in half
- 1 (12-ounce) bottle of Longboard Island Lager, or your favorite lager
- 1 bunch curly parsley, for garnish

If you're ready to make mouthwatering sea scallops intensified by butter, lemon, and an island lager, you gotta try this recipe. Best of all, it all goes down in your backyard. Because I'm a fan of big flavor and big food, you'll want to use the largest scallops you can find. I like to use U8's (meaning there's 8 scallops per pound) and I'll sear them on my Blackstone Griddle. It makes searing scallops extremely easy, but a hot skillet over coals works well too. Because scallops like to absorb any flavors you add to them, I'll go subtle on the seasoning so the natural taste of the sea shines through. Pair these succulent gems with a steak and get ready for an out of this world surf and turf.

Preheat a griddle or grill to 500°F. Add a little oil so the scallops don't stick.

Add the salt, pepper, and rub to a shallow dish and mix well.

Pat the scallops dry with paper towels then coat in the seasoning mixture (the drier they are the better the sear). Add the scallops to the preheated griddle or skillet (you should hear a loud sizzle; the sign your grill is hot). Sear about 2 minutes on one side without moving them until a golden crust forms. Turn the scallops over and place them on a new hot spot (as opposed to the same spot where they were cooking because the temperature will be lower). Sear for 1 minute, then move the scallops together in a tight circle so they're all together. Add the butter in the middle of the scallops so they cook in the butter as it melts. Squeeze the juice from half a lemon over the scallops. Then pour about 6 ounces of beer over the scallops. Remove the scallops from the grill. The internal temperature of the scallops should register 115°F. Note: The internal temperature will continue to

rise about 15°F after they're pulled off the grill. Use a scraper or spoon to collect as much of the sauce from the griddle or skillet as you can.

Transfer the scallops to a serving plate or platter. Pour the griddle sauce over the scallops and squeeze the juice from the remaining lemon half over the top. Garnish with parsley and serve.

CHAMPIONS CORNER

Experiment with different beer varieties to find the one that best suits your palate. The fun in cooking with beer lies in the subtle flavors beer can introduce to your dishes. Remember, the best dishes come from not just following recipes, but also from experimenting and adjusting to your taste preferences.

GRILLED KING CRAB LEGS WITH SEASONED GARLIC BUTTER

SERVES 4

4 pounds king crab legs (about 4 legs)

Seasoned Garlic Butter

Makes about 1¾ cups

2 lemons, halved

1½ sticks unsalted butter

2 cloves garlic, peeled

¼ cup finely chopped fresh curly parsley, plus more for garnish

⅛ teaspoon cayenne pepper

2 tablespoons sea salt

2 tablespoons fresh cracked black pepper

2 tablespoons G-Que Barbeque The Rub, or your favorite barbeque rub

For a sumptuous dining experience, this simple yet decadent recipe is for you. Try it and there's a strong likelihood you won't go back to steaming crab legs in a pot again. Douse with several brushes of my incredibly addicting Garlic Butter and these grilled crab legs will elevate any meal, be it a casual barbeque or an elegant dinner affair.

Start a chimney of lump charcoal and add the hot coals to one side of the grill (page 37).

Squeeze the lemon halves in a small foil pan. Add the butter, garlic, parsley, cayenne, salt, pepper, and barbeque rub. Mix well and place the pan over indirect heat on the grill to melt the butter. While the butter is melting, prepare the crab legs.

Using kitchen shears, cut and remove sections of the shell to expose the crabmeat. Place the crab legs, meat-side up, over indirect heat, next to the butter pan. Remember, king crab legs are already cooked when you purchase them, so you're essentially reheating them on the grill. Baste the exposed crabmeat with the Garlic Butter. Now turn the crab legs onto the hot side of the grill so the shell side is up. Baste with more Garlic Butter. When the crabmeat reaches 140°F internal temperature, remove the legs immediately from the heat and transfer to a serving platter. Finish with a drizzle of Garlic Butter, garnish with parsley, and serve.

GRILLED LOBSTER TAILS WITH GARLIC BUTTER

SERVES 4

1½ sticks unsalted butter

2 cloves garlic, peeled and finely minced

⅛ teaspoon cayenne pepper

½ cup finely chopped fresh curly parsley

Sea salt and fresh cracked black pepper, as needed

G-Que Barbeque The Rub, or your favorite barbeque rub, as needed

3 lemons, halved

4 Maine or Caribbean lobster tails

I used to receive messages over social media from home cooks and backyard grillers letting me know they'd been unsuccessful when it comes to grilling lobster tails. That was until they saw my YouTube video on how to grill lobster tails. Today, that video has garnered almost 4 million views. This is the very recipe I demonstrate in that video. Like many home cooks, I was once intimidated by grilling lobster, especially with the constant worry of overcooking or scorching the tails. Not anymore. Follow this recipe and you too will master grilled lobster at home.

Start a chimney of lump charcoal and add the hot coals to one side of the grill (page 37).

Add the butter, garlic, cayenne, and parsley to a foil pan. Season with some salt, pepper, and barbeque rub. Squeeze the juice from 2 of the lemons (4 halves) into the pan and add the rinds as well. Place the pan on the grill, opposite the coals, and let the butter melt while you prepare the lobster tails.

Using a pair of kitchen scissors, slip the scissors just under the shell at the base. Cut straight down the top of the shell towards the tail flippers, being carefully not to cut deep into the meat underneath. Once cut, you will notice sections of shell. Break the first section at the base completely off. That's because you want the lobster meat to hang over this part once the meat is propped up on the shell for presentation. Next, gently spread the shell apart and use your fingers and thumbs to loosen the meat and separate it from the shell. Work your way from the base to the flippers, keeping the meat in the flippers intact. Now carefully pull the meat out from inside the shell, use your fingers to close the shell and

lay the meat over the top. Squeeze some fresh lemon juice from the remaining lemon over the lobster tails and sprinkle a light coat of barbeque rub over the meat.

Place the lobsters on the hot side of the grill and cook for 1½ to 2 minutes per ounce. Baste the lobster meat every 1½ minutes. Note: When applying the Garlic Butter, do not brush directly on the meat or the rub will wash away. Instead, let the butter drip onto the meat. As you approach the end of your cook, be sure to check the internal temperature and remove the tails as soon as the meat registers 140°F. Any longer and the meat could seize up, giving it a tough texture.

For a garnish, take the used lemon halves and place them on the grill, face down, until charred.

Add one last drizzle of Garlic Butter, some more fresh squeezed lemon juice, and the garnish of grilled lemon halves over the lobster meat. Serve immediately.

CHAMPIONS CORNER

Cutting and lifting the lobster meat not only makes for an impressive presentation but allows the meat to cook without being scorched by the heat below. That's because the shell acts as a barrier to protect the meat. The exposed meat also absorbs the Garlic Butter much better than if it was inside the shell. Make sure to apply the Garlic Butter generously and at different stages including the last time after the lobster comes off the grill. This helps keep the lobster meat moist and flavorful.

SURF & TURF SMASHBURGER

SERVES 4

Burger Sauce

Makes about ¾ cup 2/3 cup

Miracle Whip (or mayonnaise)

2 tablespoons spicy brown mustard

1 tablespoon minced garlic

½ lemon, juiced

Salt and fresh cracked black pepper, as needed

G-Que Barbeque The Rub, or your favorite barbeque rub, as needed

Turf

1½ pounds 80/20 ground beef

Salt and fresh cracked black pepper, as needed

G-Que Barbeque The Rub, or your favorite barbeque rub, as needed

8 slices provolone cheese

4 brioche buns, split and toasted

4 green lettuce leaves, as needed

Surf

20 to 24 large raw shrimp, peeled, deveined, tails removed

2 tablespoons olive oil

4 tablespoon butter, divided

G-Que Barbeque The Rub, or your favorite barbeque rub, as needed

1 teaspoon cayenne, or to taste

½ teaspoon crushed red pepper, or to taste

½ lemon, juiced

1 teaspoon minced garlic

When it comes to eating, there's three foods I love most—surf, turf, and burgers. So, why not put all three together? That's what I did and here's the recipe. I'm using grilled succulent shrimp for the surf and juicy, meaty hamburgers for the turf. Usually, I'm not a fan of sauce on my burgers, but the Surf & Turf Burger Sauce is the perfect accoutrement for this over-the-top Smashburger.

To make the Burger Sauce: Add the Miracle Whip, mustard, garlic, and lemon juice to a bowl. Season with salt, pepper, and the barbeque rub. Whisk until combined and refrigerate until ready to use.

Preheat the griddle to high heat.

Divide the beef into 8 equal portions and form into balls. When the grill is at temperature, add the beef to one side of the griddle and smash them down with a metal spatula. Season the top of the burgers with some salt, pepper, and barbeque rub.

On the other side of the griddle, add the olive oil and half of the butter. When the butter is melted and the oil is hot, add the shrimp. Season the shrimp with the barbeque rub, cayenne, and red pepper flakes. Flip the shrimp over and continue to cook. Add the remaining butter, lemon juice, and garlic over the shrimp.

Return to the burgers and flip them. There should be a nice, dark crust that formed while the burgers were cooking. Add a slice of provolone to each burger. Next, rub the hamburger buns in some of the garlic butter from the shrimp, then toast the buns until golden brown.

Toss the shrimp one final time, then remove from the griddle, along with the buns and burgers. To assemble, add some of the Burger Sauce to the bottom of each bun, followed by a lettuce leaf. Add two burger patties to each bun. Divide the shrimp evenly and top each burger with 5 to 6 shrimp. Drizzle any remaining shrimp sauce from the griddle over each burger and top with the remaining bun halves.

CHAMPIONS CORNER

The 80/20 beef blend is key for juicy burgers. The fat renders down during grilling, keeping the patties moist and flavorful. Meanwhile, the shrimp sauce adds a delicious component to the meat, so don't forget to save all that saucy goodness from the griddle and drizzle it on top of the shrimp, letting it cascade down onto the patties.

HEIRLOOM VEGETABLES & FRESH FRUITS

When it comes to barbeque, vegetables and fruits often take a backseat, but this chapter brings them to the forefront with recipes that are as bold and flavorful as anything that comes off the grill. Grilling enhances the natural sweetness of fruits and gives vegetables a deliciously charred edge, turning even the simplest ingredients into showstoppers. Whether it's the bright, citrusy flavor of Grilled Asparagus with Lemon or the smoky depth of Bacon Fried Corn, grilling and barbeque techniques make these dishes shine in unexpected ways.

One of the undeniable stars of this chapter is the Volcano Bacon Potatoes. These eye-catching potatoes are not only a feast for the eyes, but they also explode with flavor—crispy bacon wrapping around tender, fluffy potatoes with a melted cheese center that erupts with every bite. It's a dish that's sure to turn heads at any barbeque.

From tangy Grilled Tomatillo Salsa to sweet and smoky Grilled Mixed Fruit, this chapter is packed with recipes that highlight how well fresh, heirloom vegetables and fruits take to the grill. Whether you're using them as sides, toppings, or even main dishes, these recipes will help you transform everyday produce into something truly special and unforgettable.

BACON-FRIED CORN

SERVES 6 TO 8

- 1 pound thick-sliced hickory smoked bacon, chopped
- 2 pounds fresh or frozen corn kernels, thawed
- 2 tablespoons minced garlic
- 1 small red bell pepper, cored and chopped
- 1 tablespoon G-Que Barbeque The Rub, or your favorite barbeque rub
- 1 teaspoon crushed red pepper flakes

When I'm having friends or guests over for a barbeque whom I've never cooked for before, I like to stick to ingredients that people generally like, such as grilled corn and bacon, which make a delectable duo. Blending smoky and savory flavors with a hint of sweet heat, this dish is always a hit at summer barbeques or cozy indoor gatherings. The charred kernels burst with caramelized goodness, complementing the crispy, salty allure of bacon, along with the bell pepper. Sometimes I'll serve this under a protein, like my Tequila Lime Grilled Shrimp (page 242).

Prepare the griddle to medium heat.

Add the chopped bacon to the hot griddle and cook until the bacon is slightly crispy, but not burnt. Cooking times will vary, but the bacon should be done in 7 to 10 minutes. Add the corn, garlic, and peppers and mix with the bacon. Cook for 5 minutes. If the corn is hot, add the barbeque rub and pepper flakes. If the corn is still cool or lukewarm, allow the corn to cook for several more minutes, or until hot. Remove from the griddle and serve immediately.

CHAMPIONS CORNER

The balance of flavors is key in this dish, sweet from the corn and savory from the bacon. Don't hesitate to add other items you like, such as jalapeño, lime juice, honey, or cheese. Whatever ingredients you add, add them sparingly to ensure they complement the corn rather than overwhelm it.

COOLER CORN

MAKES 24 EARS OF CORN

2 dozen ears of corn, husks and silk removed

3 sticks of unsalted butter (or 1 stick per 8 ears)

Kosher salt, as needed, to taste

One of the great advantages of cooler corn is that the corn can stay warm for a couple of hours, making it perfect for parties where guests serve themselves over time. While buttered, salted water is all you need, you can experiment with other flavors. Consider adding a cup of milk, sugar, or herbs like bay leaves or thyme for a subtly flavored corn. Make sure to use a hard-sided cooler. The cooler should not be too large; a snug fit for the corn means less water needed while keeping the corn hotter longer.

Here's a quick and easy recipe to make a bunch of corn on the cob for your next large gathering or barbeque. All you need is a cooler and a way to boil water. When I make Cooler Corn at home, I like to offer a variety of butters and spreads to pair with the corn. Herb butter, garlic butter, or even a spicy lime and chili butter are my favorites. These will elevate the corn from simple to spectacular. For those worried about BPA (bisphenol-A): Coolers are made from either polypropylene (in the cheaper coolers) and polyethylene (in the more expensive coolers). Neither of these plastics contain BPA, so it can be assumed that pretty much all coolers are unlikely to contain BPA.

Begin by cleaning your cooler. Ensure the cooler is clean and rinsed out. Place the ears of corn into the cooler, arranging them so they will be completely submerged in water. Next, bring a large pot (or multiple pots) of water to a boil. You'll need enough boiling water to completely cover the corn in the cooler. Carefully pour the boiling water into the cooler, ensuring all the corn is submerged. Add the butter and season with salt. Close the cooler lid tightly. Let the corn sit for about 45 minutes. Start checking the corn after 45 minutes. The exact time can vary based on the amount of corn, the size of the cooler, and how much water you use. The corn should be bright yellow, hot, and tender to the touch. Carefully open the cooler, and check if the corn is tender and cooked to your liking. Use tongs to remove the corn and serve immediately, or let the corn remain in the hot water to stay warm until ready to serve.

FIRE-ROASTED CORN WITH GARLIC BARBEQUE BUTTER

SERVES 6

- 6 ears sweet yellow corn, husks removed
- ¼ cup canola oil
- 2 sticks (1 cup) unsalted butter
- 1 tablespoon minced garlic
- 1 teaspoon G-Que Barbeque The Rub, or your favorite barbeque rub
- Salt and fresh cracked black pepper, as needed
- Curley parsley, as needed, for garnish

CHAMPIONS CORNER

Boost the flavor of your grilled corn by offering a "corn bar" featuring a variety of toppings. Similar to a Bloody Mary bar, offer accoutrements such as lime wedges, Cotija or Parmesan cheese, chili powder, and a selection of fresh herbs. This offers your guests the opportunity to customize their corn to their liking.

Fresh corn is one of summer's treats, and it pairs wonderfully with barbeque. When selecting corn, look for ears with bright green, snugly fitting husks, and golden-brown silk. Fresh corn should have plump, shiny kernels that feel firm to the touch. I find the best way to prepare corn is to remove the husks and grill the corn directly over a bed of hot coals. This brings out the natural sweetness of the corn, enhanced by the grill flavor from the charcoal. In my experience, cooking corn in foil or in the husk results in more of a steamed and not grilled corn. I'll then elevate the grill flavor by basting the corn with Garlic Barbeque Butter for a sensational summer treat.

Start a chimney of lump charcoal and add the hot coals to one side of the grill (page 37).

Brush the ears of corn with oil (making sure to hit every kernel) and place in the middle of the grill with the thicker end of the cobs toward the heat. While the corn is cooking, add the butter, garlic, and barbeque rub to a saucepan and place on the cool side of the grill. After about 7 minutes, add another coating of oil to the corn (this will help prevent the corn from charring too quickly). After 10 minutes, the kernels should be getting soft. Move the corn to the hot side while rotating the corn often with tongs to get some good color on each side. When well-colored, move the corn to the cool side of the grill. With a basting brush, brush the Garlic Barbeque Butter on the corn while still on the grill. After 3 to 5 minutes, remove the corn and transfer to a serving platter. Brush again with the Garlic Barbeque Butter, season the corn with some salt and pepper, garnish with parsley, and serve.

GRILLED ASPARAGUS WITH LEMON

SERVES 4

1 pound fresh asparagus

2 tablespoons olive oil

Salt and fresh cracked black pepper, as needed, to season

Grated fresh Parmesan cheese, as needed, optional

1 lemon, cut into wedges, for serving

When shopping for asparagus, look for firm, bright green asparagus with tightly closed tips. Thicker stalks are better for grilling as they hold up well to the heat and retain a satisfying texture. Experiment with different seasonings to match the asparagus with the rest of your meal. A sprinkle of crushed red pepper can add a pleasant heat, while a dash of balsamic vinegar before serving offers a sweet and tangy note.

I find grilling asparagus lifts this humble vegetable up to gourmet status. Its slender spears, lightly charred and caramelized, boast a delicious crunch with each bite. No wonder my family enjoys them so much. When grilling asparagus, the charcoal and heat intensify the vegetable's natural sweetness while infusing a smoky essence, making them even more delicious. Seasoned simply with olive oil, salt, and pepper, grilled asparagus evokes a rustic charm that complements any meal. Its vibrant green hue, meanwhile, adds a pop of color to the plate, adding to the savory experience.

Rinse the asparagus and dry thoroughly. Trim the tough ends by cutting off the ends where they naturally break. Transfer the asparagus to a sheet pan and drizzle them with the olive oil. Roll the asparagus to coat. Then season with salt and pepper.

Start a chimney of lump charcoal and add the hot coals to one side of the grill (page 37).

Arrange the asparagus perpendicular to the grill grates to prevent them from falling through. Grill for 3 to 5 minutes on each side, depending on the thickness of the asparagus. The goal is to char the asparagus slightly while keeping that delightful crunch. Remove the asparagus from the grill and arrange them on a serving platter. If desired, sprinkle grated fresh Parmesan cheese over the warm asparagus for a savory finish. Garnish with lemon wedges on the side, which offers guests a burst of lemony freshness to the asparagus taste.

GRILLED TOMATILLO SALSA

SERVES 8 TO 10

- 1 pound tomatillos, husked and halved
- 1 small white onion, peeled and halved
- 2 jalapeños, halved and seeded
- 2 garlic cloves, unpeeled
- ¼ cup vegetable oil plus 2 tablespoons, divided
- 2 tablespoons fresh lime juice
- Kosher salt and fresh cracked black pepper, as needed, to taste

Tomatillo salsa, also known as salsa verde, is a vibrant and tangy salsa. Grilling the tomatillos adds a char-grill flavor that pairs incredibly well with any smoked or grilled protein, as well as tacos, or simply enjoyed with a bowl of tortilla chips and a margarita. This is also my go-to salsa for breakfast tacos with any leftover barbeque meat.

Preheat the grill using two-zone cooking (page 30).

Add the tomatillos, onion, jalapeños, garlic, and ¼ cup oil to a large skillet. Toss well and place over the medium to medium-high part of the grill. Cook the vegetables, stirring occasionally, until slightly softened and charred in spots, 10 to 15 minutes. Remove from the heat and let cool slightly. Once cooled, peel the garlic cloves and transfer all the contents to a food processor or blender and pulse until coarsely chopped. Add the lime juice and the remaining 2 tablespoons of oil and pulse until your desired consistency. Season with salt and pepper and serve warm or at room temperature.

CHAMPIONS CORNER

Select firm tomatillos with a bright green color and tight husks. The husks should be dry, but the fruit inside should be moist. Adjust the spiciness of the salsa by the number of jalapeños and whether you include the seeds. For a very mild salsa, use just one jalapeño and remove all the seeds. Store the salsa in an airtight container in the refrigerator. The flavors will meld and develop further after a day or two.

VOLCANO BACON POTATOES

SERVES 5

- 5 large russet potatoes, washed
- Canola oil, as needed
- 20 strips thick-cut bacon, divided
- G-Que Barbeque The Rub, or your favorite barbeque rub, as needed
- ½ cup sour cream
- 2 tablespoons G-Que Barbeque Hottish Sauce, or your favorite barbeque sauce
- Hot sauce, optional
- 2 to 3 tablespoons melted butter
- 1 cup freshly shredded cheddar cheese, divided
- ¼ cup freshly grated Parmesan cheese
- 1 bunch green onions, finely sliced for garnish

Volcano Bacon Potatoes are not just a delicious and filling dish, they're an experience. With their explosive flavor and dramatic presentation, they're guaranteed to be a conversation starter at your next dinner party. Kids love them too. Enjoy the blend of textures and tastes as these potatoes, enveloped in a smoky aroma, produce a crispy skin that gives way to a fluffy, perfectly cooked interior. Nestled within are savory bites of melted cheese and crispy bacon, adding a satisfying crunch and a rich, indulgent taste. Make these fun potatoes at home and discover a delectable comfort food that satisfies the palate with an eruption of joy and deliciousness.

Poke some small holes in the potatoes to allow the steam to escape. Then slice 1 inch off one end of each of the potatoes so they can stand upright. Lightly coat the skins with the oil. Set aside.

Prepare the drum smoker to 350°F.

When the smoker is ready, stand the potatoes upright on one side of the smoker. On the other side, add 5 strips of bacon and season with the barbeque rub. Smoke the bacon for 3 or 4 minutes, then flip and season the other side. Once the bacon is crispy, about 10-15 minutes, remove the bacon from the smoker, drain, then crumble and reserve for the potato filling.

While the potatoes continue to smoke, create the lava topping by adding the sour cream and barbeque sauce to a bowl. Mix well to combine. To make your potatoes truly volcanic, add a small amount of your favorite hot sauce to the bowl and mix to combine. Set aside.

When the potatoes are soft to the touch, about 45 minutes, remove them from the grill and let cool slightly. While the potatoes are cooling, lay the remaining 15 strips of bacon in 3 sets of 5 slices, overlapping slightly each piece. Then gently roll the potatoes over the bacon strips to wrap tightly. Brush a light coating of barbeque rub over the bacon and secure with toothpicks.

Return the potatoes to the smoker, now with the cut/flat side up, for 3 or 4 minutes, or until the bacon is 90% finished. Next, brush a thin layer of barbeque sauce on the bacon and return to the smoker for 5 to 7 minutes to allow the sauce to set.

Remove the potatoes from the smoker and, using a melon scooper or long-handled spoon (a bar spoon works well), carefully hollow out the potatoes, making sure not to puncture the skin, and add the potato flesh to a bowl. To this bowl, add the melted butter, ¼ cup of cheddar cheese, Parmesan cheese, and reserved crumbled bacon. Mix to combine and add the filling back inside the potato cavities. Note: You can fill the cavities using either a piping bag, spoon, or your fingers. Return the potatoes to the smoker and then top each potato with the remaining cheddar cheese. When the cheddar cheese has completely melted, remove the potatoes from the smoker and transfer to a serving platter. Top with the lava sauce. As the residual heat from the potatoes melts the sauce, the sauce will dribble down the sides of the potato giving the impression of a volcano eruption. Garnish with chopped green onion and serve.

CHAMPIONS CORNER

When selecting russet potatoes, look for large, uniform potatoes to ensure consistent cooking and easy wrapping. Have fun with the filling too. Feel free to customize the filling with different cheeses, herbs, or even bits of cooked sausage for added flavor.

GRILLED MIXED FRUIT

SERVES 6

- 1 pineapple, peeled, cored, and cut into rings
- 2 peaches or plums, halved and pitted
- 2 bananas, peeled and halved lengthwise
- 2 tablespoons melted unsalted butter
- 2 tablespoons honey plus more for garnish
- Fresh mint leaves, as needed, for garnish
- Vanilla ice cream, as needed, optional

Experiment with your favorite fruit. Almost any fruit can be grilled. The key is to use fruits that are ripe but still firm. Overripe fruit can become mushy when grilled. Also, cut your fruit into large chunks, slices, or halves. Smaller pieces are more likely to fall through the grill grates. Remember, not all fruits require the same cooking time. Start with the fruits that take longer to cook, like pineapples and stone fruits. Soft fruits, like bananas or strawberries, need less time.

Grilled fruits, such as pineapple, peaches, plums, and bananas, offer a delicious twist on traditional desserts. When exposed to the flames, their natural sugars caramelize, intensifying their sweetness and imparting a subtle smokiness. Pineapple rings develop a caramelized crust, while peaches become tender with a hint of char. Soft fruits like bananas, when grilled, turn soft and creamy while releasing their sugary juices. At home, my family and I like to enjoy grilled fruits either on their own or paired with ice cream for a refreshing and indulgent treat. Enhance your next gathering or barbeque with a cornucopia of fresh grilled fruit.

Prepare the grill for two-zone cooking (page 30).

Prepare the fruit by brushing the fruit lightly with the melted butter. This not only adds flavor but helps in caramelizing the fruits' natural sugars. Arrange the fruit on the hot side of the grill. Grill the pineapple and peaches for 3 to 4 minutes per side, or until grill marks appear and the fruit softens slightly. For the bananas, grill about 2 minutes per side. In the last minute of grilling, brush the fruit with honey to add a sweet glaze. Remove the fruit and let rest for 2 minutes. Arrange the grilled fruit on a platter. Drizzle a little extra honey over the top, garnish with mint leaves, and serve as is or with scoops of vanilla ice cream.

BLOOMING DESSERTS & SWEETS

Desserts and sweets are the perfect way to end a meal, and in this chapter, we're bringing them to life on the grill. Fire and smoke might seem unusual for desserts, but once you experience these recipes, you'll wonder why you haven't been grilling sweets all along. From the indulgent Barbequed Gooey Layer Pie, with its rich layers of coconut and graham crackers, to the fun Grilled Banana Boats, each recipe adds a new twist to classic treats.

One of the highlights of this chapter is my daughter Hollie's Chocolate Cake. It's a family favorite and something I look forward to each year on my birthday. Rich, decadent, and unforgettable—this cake is easily the best chocolate cake I have ever had.

And if you're a fan of bacon and cinnamon rolls, then you're going to fall in love with the Grilled Bacon Cinnamon Rolls. These two classic breakfast favorites are married into one perfect, smoky treat that's bound to become a new favorite.

And if you didn't know you could make an ice cream sandwich on your grill, I will show you how with barbeque Grilled Ice Cream Sandwiches, proving that dessert deserves a spot on the grill. Get ready for these blooming dessert creations!

BARBEQUED GOOEY LAYER PIE

SERVES 8 TO 10

- 18 graham crackers
- ½ cup plus 1 tablespoon unsalted butter, melted
- ½ cup semi-sweet chocolate chips
- ½ cup butterscotch chips
- ½ cup shredded coconut
- ½ cup sweetened condensed milk

Imagine layers of rich coconut and graham cracker crust interspersed with gooey chocolate and butterscotch, all infused with a subtle smoky flavor from the barbeque. This indulgent dessert is a sweet addition to any outdoor feast, combining the rustic charm of cast-iron cooking with the irresistible allure of a decadent chocolate pie.

Prepare the grill to 350°F (medium heat) with two-zone cooking (page 30).

Spray the inside of a medium-sized cast-iron pan with non-stick spray and set aside.

Add the graham crackers to a blender and pulse until finely crushed. Transfer the cracker crumbs to a mixing bowl and add the melted butter. Mix until combined then add to the prepared cast-iron pan. Using your fingers, press the crumb mixture into an even layer forming the bottom crust. On top of the crust, add the chocolate and butterscotch chips, coconut, and condensed milk. Note: It's important to add the sweetened condensed milk last because the milk will act as a barrier to prevent the coconut from burning as it cooks on the grill. Place the pan over indirect heat, cover, and cook the pie for 18 to 20 minutes, or until the coconut starts to crisp around the sides without getting burnt. Check the pie every 4 or 5 minutes and rotate the pie 180° through the cooking process for even cooking and without one side cooking more than another. Remove the pie from the grill and let cool for 5 minutes before slicing and serving.

CHAMPIONS CORNER

Experiment by customizing the toppings and gooey layers. Add nuts, different types of chocolate, or even a hint of smoked sea salt for an extra barbeque twist. Cast-iron skillets are perfect for this recipe due to their even heat distribution. Ensure your skillet is well-seasoned to prevent sticking and to enhance the flavor.

GRILLED BACON CINNAMON ROLLS

MAKES 8 ROLLS

- 1 (16-ounce) package thin-cut bacon, divided
- G-Que Barbeque The Rub, or your favorite barbeque rub, as needed
- 1 cup packed dark brown sugar, divided
- 1 (12.4-ounce) package Pillsbury Cinnamon Roll 8-Count Refrigerated Dough with Icing
- 2 tablespoons unsalted butter
- 3 or 4 drops maple extract

Bacon makes everything better and cinnamon rolls are no exception. The unexpected twist in making these mouth-watering rolls is including bacon inside and on top of the roll, then baking the rolls to golden perfection. The result is a big, fluffy bite of savory goodness thanks to the bacon along with the sweet indulgence of the cinnamon roll itself. I also like to add a little smoke to the rolls by adding a piece of hickory to the coals. If you're ready to experience the smoky saltiness of bacon against warm, sugary cinnamon, I encourage you to make this recipe. It's perfect for a decadent breakfast treat or a unique dessert for your next barbeque.

Prep an outdoor grill for two-zone cooking (page 30).

Pull 8 strips of bacon and reserve the rest for the garnish. Season the 8 strips on both sides with barbeque rub and about ½ cup of brown sugar. Place on the low (indirect) side of the grill. Add the remaining bacon slices on the indirect side and season only with the barbeque rub. Cook the remaining bacon until it's cooked about 40% of the way through, 5 to 7 minutes, before removing from the grill. Continue cooking the candied bacon over indirect heat, flipping occasionally for even cooking on both sides.

Next, unravel each piece of cinnamon roll dough and place 1 par-cooked strip of bacon in the middle of each roll. Roll the dough back into shape, keeping 1 side of the roll flush with the bacon, which will be the top of the roll. Note: Do not use two pieces of bacon per roll; the roll will end up too greasy and won't hold its shape.

Add the butter to a large pan over indirect heat until the butter is melted. Note: Depending on the size of your pan, you may need two pans to cook all the rolls. Swirl the butter around to ensure the entire bottom of the pan is coated in butter. Then place the cinnamon rolls (flush side up) in the buttered pan and return to indirect heat. Add one small piece of hickory wood over the hot coals and cook the cinnamon rolls (with the lid closed) at a grill temperature of 300°F to 350°F.

While the rolls are cooking, make the maple icing. Add the prepackaged icing that came with the rolls to another pan. To that, add the remaining ½ cup brown sugar and maple extract. Mix well and set aside.

Check on the candied bacon; when the bacon is cooked through and the brown sugar has caramelized, remove from the heat and chop into garnish-sized bits. When the cinnamon rolls are golden brown, about 15-20 minutes, remove them from the grill and ice them with the glaze. Garnish with the candied bacon and serve.

CHAMPIONS CORNER

Serve the grilled cinnamon rolls warm, ideally while they're still slightly gooey from the icing. Go ahead and experiment with additional toppings for interesting textures and flavors, such as chopped nuts, cream cheese icing, or even a sprinkle of coarse sea salt. The key to successful cinnamon rolls is managing the heat to simulate an oven environment, so always opt for indirect heat when grilling baked goods.

GRILLED BANANA BOATS

SERVES 4

4 ripe bananas

1 cup mini marshmallows

1 cup semi-sweet chocolate chips

½ cup crushed graham crackers

Sometimes after a long barbeque cook, you just want something easy to make for dessert. This recipe is delightfully simple and caps off any barbeque feast. Imagine the sweet, creamy goodness of a ripe banana combined with gooey marshmallows and rich, melted chocolate, all wrapped up in a warm, caramelized package. This easy-to-make treat is a hit with both kids and adults alike. The best part is you can make it right on the grill. It's a fun and interactive way to end your barbeque with a dessert that's both delicious and memorable.

Use ripe, but not overly ripe, bananas. They should be firm enough to hold their shape on the grill. Feel free to experiment with different toppings like peanut butter chips, caramel bits, or chopped nuts for added texture and flavor.

Prepare an outdoor grill to 350°F or medium heat.

Make a slit down the length of each banana, leaving about ½-inch at both ends uncut. Be careful not to cut all the way through the banana. Gently open the slit to create a pocket for the fillings.

Stuff the bananas with the marshmallows and chocolate chips. Use as much or as little as you like, depending on your preference. For some texture, sprinkle some of the crushed graham crackers on top for a s'mores-inspired touch.

Carefully wrap each banana in heavy-duty aluminum foil and grill over indirect (low) heat for 10 to 15 minutes, turning occasionally, until the bananas are soft, and the chocolate and marshmallows are melted and gooey. Carefully unwrap the bananas from the foil and serve.

GRILLED ICE CREAM SANDWICHES

MAKES ABOUT 12 ICE CREAM SANDWICHES

Cookie Dough

2 1/4 cups all-purpose flour

1 teaspoon baking soda

1 teaspoon kosher salt

1 cup softened unsalted butter

3/4 cup sugar

3/4 cup packed dark brown sugar

2 large eggs

1 teaspoon vanilla extract

2 cups semi-sweet chocolate chips

1 pint vanilla (or your favorite flavor) ice cream

I enjoy ice cream so much I launched a brand here in Denver called The Ice Cream Farm. In fact, I built a bunch of ice cream shops which I placed right next to or inside my G-Que Barbeque restaurants. Tasting all our delicious flavors, Salted Caramel Oreo is my personal favorite. When I began developing our ice creams and taste-tested the dairy from different farms, I quickly realized ice cream isn't much different than barbeque. If you want to make the best ice cream, you need to start with the best, all-natural ingredients, especially the dairy. Today, we continue to make our ice cream in-house at our Ice Cream Farm location in Lone Tree, then deliver the freshly churned ice cream to our other shops. This recipe, which is super easy to make at home, features the outdoor smoker and, of course, wonderful ice cream. What I like to do is toss a couple cookies onto the smoker, let 'em smoke, then add a big scoop of ice cream and sandwich it together for the best dang ice cream sandwich you could ever make in your backyard. Just make sure to let the cookies sit in the freezer for a bit before adding the ice cream so it doesn't melt so quickly.

Prepare an outdoor grill to 350°F with two-zone cooking. Add a pizza stone or greased baking sheet over the indirect part of the grill.

To make the Cookie Dough: Add the baking soda and salt to a medium bowl and sift in the flour. Set aside. In a large bowl, add the butter, sugar, and brown sugar and beat until creamy. Add the eggs one at a time to the butter-sugar mixture and mix until combined. Add the vanilla and mix. Gradually add the flour mixture and fold in the chocolate chips. Mix

until everything is combined. Note: For thicker cookies, pre-chill the dough before baking.

Scoop the cookie dough into small balls (about 1½ teaspoons each) and transfer to the preheated pizza stone or baking sheet over indirect heat. Bake the cookies for 10 to 12 minutes, or until the edges of the cookies are golden brown with a soft center. Remove the cookies from the grill and let cool. Note: To speed up the cooling process, transfer the cookies to the freezer until chilled.

To assemble: Place a large scoop of ice cream on one cookie. Top with another cookie and gently press down forming an ice cream sandwich. Enjoy immediately or wrap the sandwiches in plastic wrap and place in the freezer until ready to eat.

CHAMPIONS CORNER

If you're like me, you don't always have time to make everything from scratch when cooking for family or friends. If time is of the essence, pick up your favorite cookie dough from the grocery store and follow the package directions. Experiment with different cookie and ice cream flavors until you find your favorite.

HOLLIE'S CHOCOLATE CAKE

1 3-LAYER CAKE (ABOUT 8 SERVINGS)

3 cups all-purpose flour
3 cups sugar
1½ cups unsweetened cocoa powder
1 tablespoon baking soda
1½ teaspoons baking powder
1½ teaspoons kosher salt
4 large eggs
1½ cups buttermilk
1½ cups warm water
½ cup vegetable oil
2 teaspoons vanilla extract
1½ cups milk chocolate chips

Frosting

1½ cups softened unsalted butter
1 cup softened cream cheese
1½ cups unsweetened cocoa powder
3 teaspoons vanilla extract
7 cups powdered sugar
½ cup whole milk

This recipe, the final one in this book, is very special to me as it's the only recipe I didn't write or adapt. My 15-year-old daughter Hollie contributed this fabulous dessert. Hollie's been baking for several years now. One year she wanted to make me something for my, ahem (cough cough), 35th birthday so she whipped this up. One bite and you'll discover how good it is. The cake is a perfectly moist, three-layer chocolate cake filled with chocolate chips and topped with rich chocolate icing. She continues to make this cake for me every year. Incidentally, Hollie entered this cake into a school-wide, anything goes cooking contest and beat out more than 50 other entries and took first place. I'm so proud of her. Maybe one day she'll try her culinary hand at competition barbeque like her ol' man. She would do very well.

Preheat the oven (or outdoor smoker) to 350°F.

Grease three 9-inch cake rounds or dust with flour or cocoa powder. Alternatively, you can lightly grease them and line them with parchment paper. Set aside.

Add the flour, sugar, cocoa powder, baking soda, baking powder, and salt to the bowl of a stand mixer and, using the paddle attachment, mix on low speed until combined. Add the eggs, buttermilk, warm water, oil, and vanilla. Beat on slow speed until smooth, scraping the sides and bottom to ensure everything is mixed in. Add chocolate chips and mix until fully combined. Divide the batter evenly among the three pans (about 3 cups of batter per pan). Tap the cakes gently on the counter to allow any bubbles to rise to the top and escape. Stir the chocolate chips in the pans just before they go into the oven, so the chips don't stick to the bottom.

Bake for 30 to 35 minutes, or until a toothpick inserted into the center comes out clean. Cool the cake on a wire rack for 15 minutes, then remove them from the pans and place them on the wire rack to cool completely.

To make the Frosting: Add the butter and cream cheese to the cleaned bowl of the stand mixer and beat until fluffy, about 3 minutes. Add the cocoa powder and vanilla. Beat until just combined, about 30 seconds. Beat in the powdered sugar, 1 cup at a time. Add the milk gradually to make it spreadable but it should still be thick. Beat until the mixture resembles a frosting. Use the frosting to frost and assemble the cake or transfer to a piping bag for decorating. Once frosted, the cake should be refrigerated before serving but can remain at room temperature up to 4 hours.

CHAMPIONS CORNER

Freeze some chocolate chips for garnish. Then top the cake with the frozen chips and serve. You will enjoy the texture and additional bursts of chocolate the chips provide.

ACKNOWLEDGMENTS

To God, who has been my guide through every step of this journey. Your grace, strength, and provision have been the foundation for G-Que barbeque. Without Your guidance, none of this would be possible. All glory and honor belong to You.

To my incredible family—Heidi, my partner in every sense of the word, and the heart of our home. Your unwavering support, patience, and belief in me have carried me through the highs and lows of this journey. Tori, Hollie, Jack, and Jenna—you are the greatest joys of my life, and everything I do is inspired by the love I have for each of you. Watching you grow and achieve your own dreams fills me with pride, and I hope this book serves as a reminder that with faith, hard work, and belief in yourself, anything is possible.

To my mom, who is no longer with us, but whose love and guidance continue to shape the person I am today. To my dad, whose wisdom, hard work, and support have always been constant. I am so grateful for everything you've taught me.

To everyone who has ever walked through the doors of G-Que Barbeque, enjoyed a meal with friends and family, or shared a kind word about us—this book is as much yours as it is mine. Your support has fueled this journey, and without your loyalty and enthusiasm, G-Que wouldn't be what it is today. Each bite, each recommendation, and each visit has helped us grow into something bigger than I could have ever imagined.

Whether it was your first time, or you've become a regular, your presence at G-Que means more than you could know. Every bite you've taken, every moment spent with family and friends around our food. Thank you for choosing us, for making us a part of your moments.

To those who've told someone about G-Que—whether it was a quick recommendation or sharing a story about your experience, your word of mouth has been the backbone of our growth. We didn't have big advertising budgets, but we had something far more powerful—you. You believed in us, and because of you, more people discovered what G-Que is all about. Your support has built this brand, and for that, I am eternally grateful.

To the G-Que Team—whether you've been with us since day one or you're new to the family, you are the foundation that keeps this dream alive. The dedication, passion, and hard work you bring every day are what allow us to give our guests their best 20 minutes of the day. You've faced the challenges, embraced the grind, and contributed to a culture that goes beyond barbeque. You've helped create an environment where we don't just serve food—we serve and fight for the best in each of us. I am so proud of each one of you, and I couldn't be more grateful to have you on this journey with me.

To the remarkable individuals who have been a part of the G-Que Barbeque team, past and present—thank you for your dedication, your passion, and your relentless pursuit of creating the best 20 minutes of the day for our guests. Whether you were with us for a moment or for years, your contributions have left an indelible mark on G-Que's story. I cannot name everyone who has played a significant role in this journey, but know that your impact has been felt, and I'm forever grateful for your hard work, heart, and hustle.

Lastly, but surely not least, let me thank the literary team who helped me to get this wonderful book off the ground and get it published: Award-winning author James O. Fraioli and his outstanding company, Culinary Book Creations, who guided, supported, and worked with me throughout the entire process. Thank you, my good friend! And thank you to food photographer Ken Goodman, Alan Dino Hebel and Ian Koviak of The Book Designers, Copy Editor Varsana Tikovsky, Nicole Frail, Associate Publisher Abigail Gehring, Senior Editor Jesse McHugh, and the entire team at Skyhorse Publishing and Simon & Schuster.

Together, we've built something truly special, and I'm proud to share this journey with all of you.

With deep gratitude,
Jason

METRIC CONVERSIONS

If you're accustomed to using metric measurements, use these handy charts to convert the imperial measurements used in this book.

Weight (Dry Ingredients)		
1 oz		30 g
4 oz	¼ lb	120 g
8 oz	½ lb	240 g
12 oz	¾ lb	360 g
16 oz	1 lb	480 g
32 oz	2 lb	960 g

Oven Temperatures

Fahrenheit	Celsius	Gas Mark
225°	110°	¼
250°	120°	½
275°	140°	1
300°	150°	2
325°	160°	3
350°	180°	4
375°	190°	5
400°	200°	6
425°	220°	7
450°	230°	8

Volume (Liquid Ingredients)		
½ tsp.		2 ml
1 tsp.		5 ml
1 Tbsp.	½ fl oz	15 ml
2 Tbsp.	1 fl oz	30 ml
¼ cup	2 fl oz	60 ml
1⁄3 cup	3 fl oz	80 ml
½ cup	4 fl oz	120 ml
2⁄3 cup	5 fl oz	160 ml
¾ cup	6 fl oz	180 ml
1 cup	8 fl oz	240 ml
1 pt	16 fl oz	480 ml
1 qt	32 fl oz	960 ml

Length	
¼ in	6 mm
½ in	13 mm
¾ in	19 mm
1 in	25 mm
6 in	15 cm
12 in	30 cm

INDEX

C